FOCUS ON TISBURY 2001–2016

Farming Life in a South Wiltshire Community

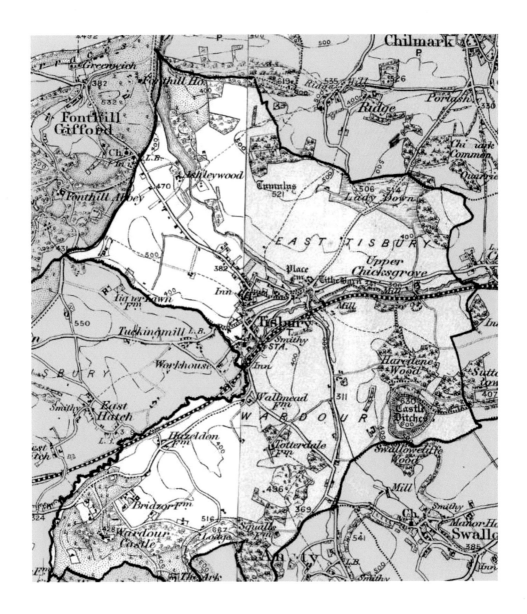

From an 1890s Ordnance Survey map. The modern civil parish boundary is superimposed. (Courtesy Wiltshire and Swindon History Centre)

Focus on Tisbury

2001–2016

_____

Martin Shallcross

First published in the United Kingdom in 2017 by Martin Shallcross

Designed by Andrew Mozley   *www.charlottemozley.co.uk*

© Martin Shallcross 2017

ISBN 978-1-9999228-0-1

Typeset in 10.5 pt Georgia

Printed by Biddles Books Ltd, Kings Lynn, Norfolk

Introduction

I live in Tisbury in the beautiful Nadder Valley in south-west Wiltshire, farming land which my father had bought in 1949. In April 2001 one of the then editors of our community magazine *Focus*, Roddy McColl, asked if I would consider producing regular articles on the theme of 'Farming in the Community'. He saw the need to inform his readers, few of whom have farming backgrounds, about what is happening around them through each season on the land.

Over the years I have followed Roddy's original intention in describing the farming year, following the many changes that have taken place in agriculture.

I have always been fascinated by the geology which underlies the land in our so-called Jurassic valley, so the Chicksgrove quarry gets several mentions. We are served by the many and varied businesses which have grown up around us and I have enjoyed interviewing many people about their origins.

I thank my wife Jenny for putting up with my monthly stints at my computer and our son Peter who manages the farms and gets up at 4.30 most mornings to milk the dairy cows.

I have kept these articles going, now over 150, and hope to continue to do so for a little while longer. Several people had asked whether they might one day be published. I'm pleased to say that Charlotte Mozley, a farmer's daughter, and her husband Andrew undertook the task of selecting articles of interest for publication.

The results of their dedication is this little book. It is graced with new photographs taken by our local photographer Jon Amos, who publishes a calendar of the village and its surroundings, and sketches by our friend Janey Alyson Smart.

Martin Shallcross
October 2017

Contents

Early days

at the farm

M y father Jack Shallcross, born in 1907, came from a clergy family. His father was the vicar of the Harptrees in the Mendips. He died when my father, an only child, was twelve. His mother used to send him to the Midlands to friends on farms for his summer holidays.

He trained as a land agent, requisitioning farms for airfields during the war. He had always wanted to farm himself. The opportunity arose in 1948 when the last Lord Arundell died at Chester on way back to Wardour from Colditz prison camp in Germany. Death duties had to be paid and several farms on the Wardour estate came on the market. My father bought a 250-acre Wallmead farm.

The farm had been let to the Doggrell family and little money had been spent on it for many years. There was no mains electricity and chickens were kept in the farmhouse, which was 18th-century and quite primitive. There were several cottages. None had indoor sanitation. The fields were mainly in grass and forty Shorthorn dairy cows were milked by two men, Fred Rogers and Jack Ingram.

Workers at Wallmead Farm in 1949

Two horses were kept by Wilf Rasen the carter and two early Fordson Major tractors were driven by the two Teds, Rixon and Woods. Ted Woods was the only one to have a car. These regular farm workers were augmented at harvest by part-timers.

Wallmead Farm is in our beautiful Nadder Valley in south-west Wiltshire. It is quite hilly and the main soil type is heavy loam over limestone. Most of the fields are the same shape as they were then. No main roads serve the nearby village of Tisbury. We have an invaluable railway station. The low railway bridge over the river Nadder keeps high lorries away but causes problems in moving large agricultural vehicles form one farm to another.

Apart from the dairy herd and the followers there were about eighty acres of cereals. Wheat and barley were harvested with a reaper and binder. The sheaves were stacked and thatched by Ted Woods. During the winter a travelling threshing machine came to thresh the ricks and the corn was stored in large sacks in an old barn, ready to be sold later.

My father continued working as a land agent and became senior partner of Rawlence and Squarey in Salisbury. The office in Rollestone Street is now occupied by the *Salisbury Journal*.

He employed a farm foreman, Bill Cornick, who lived in Haygrove on the top of the hill. There was no road to the cottage, no electricity and an intermittent water supply from the adjoining farm. Fairly soon my father built a modern house close to Jobbers Lane where successive managers lived.

When the last manager, Philip Skinner, retired my son Peter took over managing the farm, living in Haygrove which by then had been much improved.

I too trained as a land agent and have never worked physically on the farm but I still keep the books. I also followed in my grandfather's footsteps, being ordained into the Church of England in 1980. We were quite a religious farm when Philip Skinner was also ordained.

January 2013

I was at boarding school at Burnham-on-Sea when I received a message from my father to say that he had bought Wallmead Farm from the Wardour estate and we would be moving there in the spring of 1949.

My feelings were very mixed. My sister Ros and I had lived in a large house at Alderbury with eight acres of grounds and a life of luxury; much of my leisure time had been spent in visiting the signal box at Alderbury Junction where I was sometimes allowed to give the tablet to the driver, allowing his train to enter the single line section to Downton on the Salisbury-to-Bournemouth train.

My sister Ros helped with the lambs

My journey to school three times a year was also a railway adventure. My luggage was sent 'passenger's luggage in advance' and a friendly porter at Salisbury Station put me on the right train for Templecombe. From the ages of 8 to 12 I then had to change platforms to catch a Bournemouth-to-Bath train, changing trains again at Evercreech Junction. This was an exciting place with rows of engines poised to assist trains to the north like the Pines Express up the one-in gradients over the Mendip hills. To this day, I pause at the overgrown Maesbury summit on the way to Bristol airport to marvel at the engineering feats of the Somerset and Dorset railway.

From Evercreech I took the very slow line to the terminus at Burnham where the rails looked as though they would like to continue through the turbulent River Brue to south Wales.

The last stage of this journey to Burnham, immortalised by John Betjeman on a tape, could be tricky as there was no corridor and therefore no means for nervous lads to relieve themselves except at the destination. This can be a problem of old age too but did not worry Betjeman.

The only attraction about Tisbury to me at the time was that the main railway line to the south-west, then double tracked, passed through the farm. I would be able to see the *Devon Belle* going past at speed with its Pullman coaches and observation car, which has now been miraculously restored to the Swanage Railway, as well as the *Atlantic Coast Express* running on a Saturday in several sections from Waterloo to many destinations as it was divided in Devon.

However, I foresaw myself entering a life of drudgery, as agricultural life then was not unlike the Victorian farm which has recently figured on television. Mangolds and swedes were hoed by hand. There were two rather inadequate tractors, two horses and at times about ten men employed on 250 acres, all involved in manual work.

Tisbury station had a large staff. We were phoned when a truck was left in the sidings full of sacks of fertiliser for the farm. Unloading this was the worst job I had to do. I spent a complete season aged 17 taking a share in every back-breaking task until I left for agricultural college and national service.

Things were about to change and it was not long before sprays became available so that we did not have to hoe acres of root crops by hand. Combines replaced the reapers and binders. We bought more powerful tractors fitted with hydraulic apparatus which enabled them to lift weights and eventually the dreaded two-hundredweight sacks were made redundant. Milk churns were replaced by refrigerated tanks and virtually every aspect of the hard farming life of the first half of the 20th century was changed beyond recognition. Currently we are farming five times the area of land with one third of the manpower.

Looking back sixty years is rather like revisiting the Dark Ages. The imagination boggles at how farming may be in fifty years' time; we all know that the rate of change is accelerating.

The farming year

2001–2009

May 2001

I n these occasional articles I hope to give you an idea of the pattern of life on a local dairy farm throughout the seasons. May is the month for preparing food stocks for our cattle to eat next winter.

The cows have to be kept indoors from November to April as our pasture is too wet for them to walk on without damaging the turf, and in any case the grass is not growing. If you have a lawn you will know that you have to start cutting at the beginning of April and mowing becomes a weekly chore for about four months; this is the period we have been preparing for. All the grass fields are fertilised and then harrowed and rolled so that the grass can be cut cleanly without picking up the soil from mole hills that would contaminate it.

As soon as the fields are dry enough, towards the end of April, the cows go out onto new grass. You may have seen the amazing display of liberated skipping that 125 cows indulge in for the first twenty minutes or so of freedom.

Their winter quarters, buildings larger than the Sports Centre, are thoroughly cleaned out and within a couple of weeks Sidfords, our neighbouring contractors, arrive with a forage harvester and trailers to cut over a hundred acres of standing grass. This then ferments in the largest building into a thousand tonnes of sweet-smelling silage. The clamp is rolled to expel air and then sealed with a plastic sheet. Samples are taken and analysed to assess the quality of it so that a balanced ration can be worked out for the cows when they return to eat the silage in the autumn.

Even when the cows are out at grass, they need to be monitored carefully. Those who have recently calved will be at their maximum milk production yielding half their annual output of 7,000 litres in three months, averaging 35 litres (over seven gallons) a day. They are liable to suffer from mineral deficiency if minerals are not added to their feed, and the grass is supplemented by high-protein cake when they come into the milking parlour twice a day.

Foot-and-mouth regulations are in force at present. When allowed, our cows will be crossing the Wardour road again. Most people wait patiently in their cars, enjoying watching their slow passing. People who have cut it fine to catch the train sometimes display early symptoms of road rage!

Fourteen years later we are milking 220 cows with the same acreage at Wallmead Farm although we now farm a thousand acres for all our

enterprises. The extra winter food is provided by forage maize, and annual
milk yields have increased to 8,000 litres.

June 2001

L ast month I wrote about the importance of grass in feeding our dairy
cows. This month I want to discuss the other crops we grow on our
mixed farm.

The soil in the Nadder Valley is mainly classed as Grade 3. This means that
because it is thin and stony only a limited range of crops can be grown
successfully. In many fields stone is found only about nine inches below the
surface, and the topsoil is heavy and difficult to cultivate as it goes from being
too wet to too dry very quickly. Sometimes we have to sow seed directly
behind the plough.

Wheat and barley grow well but we have to plan a rotation so that the same
crop is not grown on any one field more than two years running. At least ten
per cent of the arable land has to be rested in 'set-aside' each year according
to EU regulations.

We grow beans and peas which are high-protein legumes. They are ground up
with the cereals to produce a balanced diet for the cows.

Sometimes we grow oilseed rape which is sold and crushed to make cooking
oil. It can also be used as motor fuel but this is not economic at present
because of fuel tax. Its brilliant yellow flowers add colour to the spring
countryside but some people are allergic to its pollen.

Dr John Dalton has swum dolphins (artificial) in the fields of blue lucerne but
we have found that the yields have been so low that often the crop is not
worth harvesting. So I regret that you may see little in this area this year.

June is the month when all these crops will be growing well, although many
fields were sown very late this year due to the wet winter and spring. Many
pests and diseases can severely reduce the yields of all our crops between now
and harvest. The weather is always an unknown factor which affects all our
yields. Crop walkers, called agronomists, visit us regularly so we can see
trouble coming and hopefully deal with it early on.

Next month we will be preparing for harvest.

Set-aside was replaced by 2015 by other regulations to green the countryside and improve habitats for wildlife. Linseed has virtually vanished from farms as have beans and peas in Wiltshire.

August 2001

On 6 July, Wiltshire County Council announced that, with the easing of foot-and-mouth restrictions, all public rights of way would be opened. We took down the sign reminding people that the bridleway which goes through our farmyard to Wardour was closed. Through the same post we received a 15-minute video from our new ministry called DEFRA, warning us to be vigilant and to disinfect everything that moves on or off the farm. Foot-and-mouth still rumbles away with two to four new cases a day, each a disaster for the animals and people involved.

Cattle still succeed in straying out of their fields and people stop to tell us they are on the road. Communications are vital to get a posse together to put them back. Mobile phones are the best answer but coverage in our valley is patchy; only Orange seems to answer our needs but there is no signal in the farmyard itself. I can only use my phone in the house by climbing to the attic and leaning out of the window. Imagine our delight when Vodafone wanted to hide masts in copses at both Wallmead and Teffont and even pay rent for them. Alas, the Salisbury District Council planners did not agree and now they have given up the proposal.

Water escapes as well as animals. Indeed, water to the value of £2,300 escaped from a trough into the river last winter and we were most grateful to Wessex Water for cancelling the bill. We are big spenders with them as our cattle drink £5,000 worth a year from the mains supply. They also drink river water from the ford when grazing in the field opposite our farmhouse.

A few weeks to harvest and then the arable cycle starts again. The crops have picked up after a shaky start in the winter.

© Jane Alyson Smart

September 2001

H arvest has started and will be nearly complete by the time you read this. In the Boot Inn in Tisbury High Street hangs a photograph of the dozen or so men who used to bring in the harvest at Wallmead in the 1950s. Now one combine driver and two tractor/trailer drivers do it all in air-conditioned comfort.

I have done it both ways and know which I prefer. I can still remember handling the sheaves of corn, one under each arm and the feel of the thistles on bare arms. I can remember working on the rick, stacking sheaves hour after hour, praying that the elevator would break down to give us a break.

Now our corn is promptly taken by lorry to the grain silos at Shrewton to be dried, cleaned, graded and sold later. The marketing is left to others so we don't need to worry about the corn once it has left the farm.

The third cut of grass in August finally filled our enormous clamp so now we have enough fodder for the winter. We have also made whole crop wheat into silage and crimped wheat, and crushed it to enable the cattle to digest it, to give them some variety and extra protein.

Peter, my son, has always been keen on moths and butterflies. He was pleased when an old friend recently visited with all the gear to provide strong lights after dark. They trapped over forty types of moths in one location and were not reported to the law for acting suspiciously at night. Apart from the odd poacher, few people are out late on the land to observe the multitude of nocturnal wildlife that takes over when we draw the curtains.

October 2001

H arvest was completed in the second week of September and now only 45 acres of maize stands head-high overlooking the village waiting to be made into silage later. You will have had a chance to experience a maize crop yourself if you've visited Karen Oborne's maize maze at her Ansty pick-your-own. A good crop yields 25 tonnes per acre and needs a lot of farmyard manure to make it grow.

The rainfall has been interesting this year. A total of 452mm (18 inches) fell in the first four months and 180mm (7 inches) from May to August, nearly a year's worth in six months, but we and the cows and crops have adjusted well.

We are about to rent a 200-acre farm at Chicksgrove and with it a lambing flock of 400 ewes which will doubtless be attempting to escape, when they are not trying to expire, such are the rather trying traits of sheep. We shall also get more phone calls: 'sheep on the road', 'there's one on its back'...

The lamb market is in trouble this autumn as the Welsh flock produces small lambs beloved of the French who cannot import them because of lingering foot-and-mouth problems. We hope things will improve next season when we are selling lambs ourselves. Meanwhile there are bargains in the shops and an opportunity to buy lambs direct from the hill farmers.

When we came to Wallmead in 1948 my father had a state-of-the-art milking parlour installed by Alfa Laval to replace the old vacuum pipe line with which two men, Fred Rogers and Jackie Ingram, milked forty cows into buckets. When my father retired in 1980 his last improvement was to put in a spanking new parlour in which Sadie Cooper has milked the cows, now numbering 150, for twenty years.

We are now about to start milking in a new high-tech parlour with blue fibreglass walls. This should halve milking times and generally provide better milking conditions for cow and milker. No doubt there will be teething problems.

November 2001

The new milking parlour came into use during the last week in September and worked perfectly the first afternoon. A fitter and an electrician were present throughout. We were all very happy with their work and the cows, whose anxiety could be measured by the number of cowpats at each milking, only took a day or two to adjust. Now we milk eight on each side of the operator in a wide pit instead of five and the milking clusters are removed automatically as the milk flow of each cow dries up.

The machinery works faster than we can operate it and the cows are milked so fast that they are reluctant to give way to the next batch, as they are still often eating their in-parlour feed when all the milk clusters have come off. We have a similar problem waiting for pudding at our family Sunday lunch. Anyway we will save about one hour at each milking. This gives us and the cows more time for other things.

Some of the big straw bales covering our silage clamp suddenly caught fire one afternoon early in October. Fortunately Peter was on hand to put it out almost immediately or we could have lost 800 tonnes of silage and our biggest building. We are farming in the community and not in a prison with fences to keep people out. We would not like to develop a siege mentality as some farmers on urban fringes have had to do. *

Our 350 tonnes of wheat are now safely stored in the bins built by Wiltshire Grain near Stonehenge divided into three qualities for sale over the winter.

The 100 tonnes of barley are of malting quality and so may be sold at a premium.

Our financial year ended on 30 September so everything has to be valued for stocktaking and the books closed on another year.

This has been the only case of apparent arson we have experienced and, apart from the theft of a Land Rover, we have been almost crime free.

January 2002

The farm worker, even more than the farmer, is an endangered species. A few months ago I said how few people were involved in the corn harvest these days compared with fifty years ago. We now farm a thousand acres in the Nadder valley. The physical work is done by just three full-time people: Peter Shallcross assisted by Sadie in the dairy and Allan Porter on his tractor. Part-timers help in the winter and Sidfords contracting team provide lots of men and machines for concentrated tasks such as grass and maize silage. Looking after animals needs much more labour than arable farming. Velcourt, international farm management consultants, farming the Fonthill estate land, need only three men to farm a much greater arable acreage. As you can imagine, these men are highly trained to handle very expensive machinery.

Tractor drivers work in air-conditioned cabs with complete sound systems and can be recruited only with some difficulty. However, it is now almost impossible to find experienced milkers. Starting work at 5am and finishing at 7pm is not everyone's dream and no one has yet automated the cow's digestive system. The Irish dairy industry has a similar problem which they are solving by recruiting from the former Soviet Baltic states such as Latvia. Last year over 18,000 non-EU workers were given permits to work in Eire in a variety of industries. Our government does not allow this.

I can remember managing a dairy near Andover nearly thirty years ago where the cows were milked by a single Latvian who had escaped the Russians after the war. He was a highly motivated and pleasant man who played table tennis to a high standard when not attending to his Guernsey herd. His wife and daughter could not join him so he sent most of his wages home.

In 1954, 157 people were employed by the Morrison family on the Fonthill estate in a wide range of duties, mainly on the farms. Today 18 work on the estate including the three with Velcourt. However, the policy of converting redundant farm buildings to non-agricultural use and letting them has resulted in 121 more people being based there. If this continues there will soon be more jobs at Fonthill than fifty years ago. I am grateful to Simon Fowler, agent for the Fonthill estate, for this information.

With the expanded European Union we have been able to accept workers from Poland and the other new entrant countries since 2014. As a result we had an excellent Polish tractor driver working for us for several years. He and his wife, concerned by Mr Cameron's posturing about leaving the EU, have become naturalised British subjects.

February 2002

We have started the New Year with major problems for the livestock industry as we are still coping with the aftermath of two major diseases. The largest foot-and-mouth epidemic in history hit the country last March; fortunately there were no cases in south Wales, Dorset or Hampshire. However, livestock markets are still closed so it is very difficult to establish the value of calves, store cattle and sheep which are all normally sold in this way. We are still very restricted in moving livestock from farm to farm. The disease only affects cloven-hooved animals so it seemed surprising that American and other tourists were reputedly refusing to eat English breakfasts in their B and Bs in case they caught it.

However the first epidemic was Bovine Spongiform Encephalopathy (sorry!), commonly referred to as BSE or mad cow disease. It peaked in early 1993 and affected nearly every dairy farm in the country. Our first case was in 1988 and the last in 1997. Only the affected cows were slaughtered. The disease has virtually run its course in this country but continues to crop up in cows in France where the whole herd is destroyed if one case is found. As a precaution in the UK, no cattle over thirty months old now go into the food chain so all our retired cows are cremated.

The beef market, which was already weak, received another blow because there were forecasts of hundreds of thousands of cases of variant CJD possibly occurring in the human population. This now seems like hundreds, making it a very low-risk disease, though a most unpleasant one. There is virtually no market for crossbred heifer calves; some are shot at birth but not by us.

Food and drink scares are a favourite preoccupation with journalists and have strange results. Some people believe that bottled water is better than Wessex Water's product delivered to the tap of every household at a metered cost of 1p per litre. French water in the supermarket costs between 44.5 and 59.33 pence per litre. We produce milk containing only four per cent butterfat and we get 21 pence per litre. Half or more of the fat is removed and you pay 62.5 pence per litre.

Others think that food labelled 'organic' is healthier and tastes better than food grown in the normal way. The Advertising Agency has had to rap the knuckles of the Soil Association, which makes such unproven claims. However, if people are prepared to pay more for it, who am I to complain as long as the British farmer or grower benefits and it is not flown halfway around the globe?

Next month the ground may be dry enough for us to do some fieldwork again.

The situation about buying water and the equivalent cost of milk remains the same 13 years later in 2015. We receive little more for our milk as it is a loss-leader in the supermarkets. Most of the smaller dairy farmers have given up.

May 2002

I was recently given a very large and heavy block of 750 pages of aerial photographs and maps of the whole of England. The photos were taken at a height of 5,000 feet to a scale of 1:72,000. Groups of houses can be picked out, but part of the interest to me was the intricate patchwork of thousands of fields, all fitting together like a gigantic jigsaw puzzle with only the coastline as a border. Each of those fields is farmed, each is unique in its own way; what a precious heritage to record in this way as a millennium project. The predominant colour was of course green and now grass is growing strongly in all those fields so that they must soon be grazed with livestock or cut for silage or hay if they are not to spoil.

Our dairy herd will be out all the time, except during milking, by the time you read this. As I write there is a cold east wind and frost at night so we are keeping them in as we have plenty of silage for them.

Our 400 ewes lambed about 800 lambs which you may see cavorting around beyond Chicksgrove. The lambing took place within a few weeks in March with expert help for which we are most grateful. Sheep do not like being in the lambing shed for long, so even the smallest lambs were soon outside.

At this time of year, farmers with few buildings but lots of grass go to the store cattle auctions which have now restarted since many of the restrictions imposed during the foot-and-mouth epidemic have been lifted. We were glad sellers in March of about thirty crossbred steers and heifers – glad because the buyers seemed to have spring fever! You may remember that I mentioned recently that some dairy farmers were disposing of their crossbred heifer calves at birth because they had no potential value, but that we were keeping ours. I think it paid off as our 12- to 16-month-old heifers made £212 each and must have made a small margin over the cost of keeping them; by contrast their brothers sold for between £335 and £426. I don't envy anyone trying to make a living from heifer calves at that price, but all that green grass has to be used.

November 2002

What wonderful weather we had in September. All the month's rain fell in 24 hours and freshened up the stubble so, with the aid of a new seed drill, we were able to sow all the winter corn and re-seed some grassland by the second week in October. The forage maize matured early, so that was cut and clamped at the end of September. It smells good enough to eat, even for me, but I won't deprive the cows.

Our bull calves only make £10 each in the market and we need to breed lots of good heifers from our best cows in order to improve the genetics of the dairy herd. We were delighted that one of our best cows produced healthy twin heifer calves last week having been mated, by insemination, to a premium bull. Twins are at risk because, in cattle, if the calves are one of each sex, the female is infertile and of little value. It is now possible to pay more and buy sexed semen but it costs more and the results are not guaranteed. They can be reminiscent of Southampton FC's games at the beginning of each season!

I have been checking the Countryside Agency's website to see the extent of open land that has just been designated at the draft stage for public access rights. It includes all land previously registered as common land, like Semley Common, and additional areas which, in South Wilts, appears to be mainly very steep downland such as the slopes to the south of the A30. I understand that, if the draft map is approved, Madonna who lives near Tollard Royal may be overlooked by picnickers in spite of the measures she has taken to improve security. Woods are excluded from open access as is most arable land. During the summer, and near livestock, dogs must be kept on leads not more than two metres long. There will be no additional rights to ride horses or bikes or drive vehicles on the new open land, nor a right to camp, hang glide or to use a metal detector. I could not see any designated land in the parishes of Tisbury or West Tisbury.

The weather has just started to turn, pumpkins are about to be weighed and autumn is here.

January 2005

For weeks the farm, and indeed the village, have been bracketed by Countryside Alliance posters urging us to 'Fight Prejudice'. One at the top of Jobbers Lane seems to demand a response from me every time I pass it. What sort of prejudice should we be fighting?

At the end of the 19th century our rural society was clearly defined, and possibly divided, by class. Mrs Alexander's hymn 'All things bright and beautiful' was written at that time and contained the famous verse 'The rich man in his castle, the poor man at his gate, God made them high or lowly and ordered their estate'.

This is included in the hymn book given by my grandfather George, rector of East Harptree on the Mendips, to his wife Ethel on 1st June 1916. He was quite an elderly bridegroom and died when my father Jack was 12. A little later, in the aftermath of the First World War, class differences began to level although for many years afterwards the bowler hat and a flat cap were visible signs of social status. My father was a flat cap man but always wore a bowler for serious occasions, such as going to London or attending funerals. The verse was dropped from the revised version of *Hymns Ancient and Modern*, through an early example of political correctness, about 50 years later.

However, before the turn of the 19th century that gadfly of society, Oscar Wilde, included in a play the line 'You should study the peerage..... it is the best thing in fiction the English have ever done'. The better-known quote which followed was 'The English country gentleman galloping after a fox.... the unspeakable in full pursuit of the uneatable'. I can remember a rather truncated version of this being quoted to me at an early age. So prejudice was perhaps class prejudice until some decades ago. Is this what the placards are urging us to fight? Possibly but unlikely. If not, I assume that the prejudice is between city dwellers with mainly Labour MPs and country folk with Tory MPs, a battle hopefully to be fought with words between reasonable people. We have to remember that civilised conversation is only possible between those who agree to treat each other as equals. I doubt if this is possible between those who hold to determined views at either end of the divide, particularly with regard to blood sports.

My own enquiries in searching out prejudice among anti-hunting people reveal a deeply felt dislike of hunting with dogs on three grounds: a repugnance towards the concept of artificially encouraging one animal to pursue another to death; the unfairness of the odds of hounds to fox of perhaps 40 to 1; and the dismay that otherwise compassionate humans should obtain pleasure from this. For them it is at heart a matter of animal rights. This is an enormous subject embracing other field sports and indeed the business of keeping livestock for meat, particularly so-called factory farming. Is this prejudice and, if it is, how can we fight it? The placard poses a question every time I drive past.

We who depend on our living from the land have other battles to fight too. For us dairy farmers it is the price of milk in the supermarkets. More of that another time.

July 2005

Now that we farmers are no longer encouraged to produce food, we have to adjust in various ways to our role of custodians of the countryside. We have already entered various schemes to preserve wildlife. We leave field margins uncultivated, we plant hedges and encourage wildlife habitats. These are now to be rolled into new 'stewardship schemes': entry-level and higher-level both involving more form filling. An army of civil servants check the forms and they work for several countryside quangos. These are to be amalgamated into one body called Natural England. It is possible that the number of their employees will outnumber farmers.

Thinking about this as I hoed my garden vegetables in the cool of the late evening after a recent hot day, I mused on the relationship between man, his modified domestic animals and the true wildlife around me. Two squadrons of rooks flew in from the south in their hundreds, probably from feeding on the just-emerging maize plants in Chantry Field. They settled noisily to roost in the alder trees along  the river. A red-legged partridge made a noise like a rusty gate every few minutes as he watched over his mate sitting on her eggs under the hornbeam hedge, undisturbed by my earlier hedge trimming. Under the old carpet covering my compost heap, a toad moved lazily to catch an insect.

The milk tanker slowed to turn into the yard to collect the day's milk. The lambs in the meadow bleated in despair, having strayed from their mothers. When I went to agricultural college in Devon, I learnt new regional words for young ewes: gimmers, hoggs or hoggets, and tegs. Around us here they were called chilvers. The excellent book *Dialect in Wiltshire* published by the Wiltshire County Council in 1987 shows that 'chilver' is a very local name indeed, being known in an area only about fifty miles by ten. It has been preserved here for at least 800 years, but is it still in use?

I digress and return to my comparison of man and unmodified nature. My peace is shattered by a motorcycle engine suddenly being opened up to full throttle in the village beyond the railway line. I thought about endangered species and suddenly realised that Man, the most recent of all the species around me, is possibly the most endangered. The soil and its natural inhabitants are neutral; Man is self-destructive. In thousands of years' time the rooks and toads will still be going through their own undemanding life cycles without the benefit of carpet or compost heap – unless of course we have finished them off too.

October 2005

At the end of September it is time to put our rams out with the ewes. They have to be young and fit, as each will have to serve about a hundred ewes in two or three weeks. They then have the rest of the year to recover without female company. This year we have bought four young Texel rams from Mere costing £320 each. The economics of breeding any pedigree animals works like a pyramid. The peak of the Texel pyramid can be found at the August sales at Lanark.

This year 335 ram lambs, born this spring, averaged £2,200 each. The top price was 44,000 guineas, the traditional way of selling important livestock at auction, one guinea is now £1.05 paid by a syndicate of three breeders! Several more made over 20,000 guineas. We only sell our lambs for meat, so we are at the broad base of the pyramid together with most of the 40,000 farmers who are registered with the British Wool Marketing Board and need to buy rams each year. It is a big and demanding business; very few make these top prices.

Incidentally I am no judge of dogs but I was interested to see the great variety of Tisbury dogs who came to the recent show at the South Western Hotel. There was sadly no class for the fastest local canine. If there had been, my shirt would have been on Chloe. She lives in Court Street and races the 9am down-train, now non-stop, along Fry's Meadow. It is an awesome sight and can be viewed from the 8.48am up-train waiting in the loop.

I mentioned last month that all English elms seem to be descended from one tree and the same may be true for dogs. The rest is down to crossbreeding. I saw recently that almost all modern racehorses can be traced to a four-year-old Arab colt brought to this country by our consul in Syria, Thomas Darley, in 1704. Perhaps it would be worth going to Lanark next year to buy the champion and try to get to the peak of the Texel pyramid.

There has been just enough rain post-harvest to allow ploughing to proceed well and grass to be re-sown after cereal stubbles. There is no sign of any better prices for the stored wheat and the price of fertiliser has rocketed as the cost of natural gas, from which it is made, has tripled in five years. This will justify new gas fields in the East being brought into play and the price may be reduced, otherwise the growing of arable crops on our grade of land will be even more unprofitable.

I realise that my take on the outlook for European farming has been very pessimistic recently, so I thought I would interview some of our farming neighbours and give you their views over the winter months. Perhaps they can see a silver lining somewhere in the clouds.

September 2007

It was January that I last reported on our own farm. What a strange seven months of weather. The year started as usual with three wet months followed by an April with virtually no rain and then 440mm (half a year's rain) in the three months to the end of July. This meant that the spring-sown corn looked as though it would fail. But it didn't! There was no chance to make any hay in June or July, and by the time we had dry weather in August the grass was of poor feeding value. It was just as well that we gave up relying on hay twenty years ago. We kept making grass silage all summer, thanks to our contractors Sidfords and the big machines they brought in every time there was an odd dry day. We will have sufficient winter fodder for the dairy cows when the fodder maize has been clamped.

Come August the sun shone and the rain stopped for a week enabling our faithful yellow combine harvester, now nearly twenty years old, to cut the oats, then the barley, followed by the wheat and then more barley in about ten days. As we have only one full-time employee, Allan Porter, who is the combine driver, we took on a Polish man who was brought up on a farm and likes working a 15-hour day. We also hired a CAT material handler for two months so that, with casual labour and using our contractors to bale, we could load straw bales quickly and got them under cover before it rained for the Shaftesbury and Gillingham show week.

Two years ago we were getting about £65 a ton for our wheat, last year it was £85 and this year it looks like £140. That is great but we are now only where we were 12 years ago! Hopefully the lean years are over for a while. The reason for the jump in price is the increasing use of cereals for the production of ethanol to replace fossil fuels and also world-wide seasonal effects on yields. Even if all the corn (maize) production in the USA was switched to produce ethanol, it would only satisfy 12 per cent of America's gasoline needs. The case for using food crops for this purpose is, to my mind, dubious as fossil fuels have to be used to produce the vast quantities of fertiliser needed to grow corn economically.

Increases in the world price of wheat will make intensive livestock, pigs and poultry more expensive for the better-off who can afford to buy meat, but an extra 16 million people will become 'food-insecure' for every one per cent rise in world staple food prices.

There is real hope that we are about to be paid at least for the cost of production of the 1.2 million litres of milk we produce yearly, instead of working at a loss. This would be really good news. On a lighter note, it is interesting to compare the temperaments of breeds of cow in our herd from different countries. The few Swiss Brown cows tend to be responsible leaders of our herd and everyone thinks they look pretty. One hundred and fifty British Friesians form the core, unexciting but reliable. They have been rather put out by the arrival of ten in-calf Montpelier heifers from France via East

Stour. They have black bodies and white faces so they look like Herefords crossed with Friesians. They are unpredictable and flighty. The peace has been rather disturbed by these Gallic additions, and I for one can't quite understand them: *entente cordiale* has not yet been reached.

June 2008

T he Wessex Water meter reader comes round in May and I predict that this year about 10,000 cubic meters will have been used on the four farms at a cost of about £16,000.

We have connected the four houses at Wallmead direct to the mains, so now we are about to pump water from the adjacent River Nadder for the cows, the main users. For decades they have been drinking from the ford in the river when they are grazing the Railway Meadow and there is no health risk. We hope to make a good saving.

The Environment Agency have given grants to us and our neighbours upstream to fence the river on both sides to stop the banks being trodden by livestock – a mixed blessing for fishermen – and also to concrete areas where the cattle walk so they can be kept clean to minimise dirty run-off. The river should therefore be marginally cleaner.

The ducks have been experiencing a poor breeding season at Wallmead. One light-coloured mother proudly visited our front lawn about four weeks ago with 15 babies which shrank to two within three days and then failed to materialise again. Billy my grandson and I walked the river banks to see if we could find any nests. We eventually spotted one nearly white duck sitting very confidently close to the river's edge. She got up and we found she was trying to hatch a rather bald tennis ball that must have floated down in the floods!

May has been a scramble. Nearly a hundred acres of land have been ploughed, worked down to a fine tilth and sown to forage maize which will be in the silage pits at the end of September, a very short growing season. A stony field at Wardour was ploughed, prepared and sown to turnips for the sheep all in one day so that the loss of precious moisture in the soil is minimised. Last year these small seeds failed to germinate as we had no rain at all in April. A deluge at the very end of this April may have done the trick for us but more rain is needed. The first cut of grass silage is now due and will leave freshly mown fields for the Wiltshire Wildlife farm visit which is about to happen.

Our neighbours, the Frys of Totterdale, have got rid of their cattle for now. Our sheep flock competes with the dairy cows for grazing so we are temporarily taking over some of the fields the Frys occupy and putting some of our sheep into them. Sheep, like all animals, only thrive with regular changes of grazing. This will enable more of our arable land to be sown with wheat next year and then re-sown to grass.

You would think that, with current world shortages, Tisbury should be surrounded with fields of wheat but a good yield can only be obtained in the first, or possibly the second, year on better soils. Then the land has to be rested using a 'break crop' which is often oilseed rape, now in demand for oil substitution in fuels as well as its primary use in cooking oil. We find this difficult to grow successfully so we use barley, oats and grass for our break crops.

The price of phosphate fertiliser has rocketed so we are now buying Fibrofos in 25-ton loads. It comes from a power station at Ipswich. It is the ash left over when chicken manure has been burnt to generate electricity. A good example of recycling, but I wonder what it is like to live downwind of the power station.

October 2008

This year has proved to be the most difficult for harvesting for many years. The rainfall over the last ten weeks has been well over 300mm. Last year 164mm fell in this period, nearly all in July, and in 2006 a normal 120mm enabled most of the corn to be stored at below 15 per cent moisture without having to dry it.

The Frys' two new combines can harvest up to a hundred acres of wheat a day. A total of 2,500 acres were lined up for them but the most each has managed is sixty acres a day, and that very infrequently. If the grain goes into the trailer at over 22 per cent moisture it may need to be dried twice, something that the giant store at Wiltshire Grain cannot do. Matt and Daniel Fry have been working nightshifts to dry their neighbours' corn at Totterdale. They have been spending £20,000 a month on oil to fire the drier. The end is nowhere in sight; I write halfway through September as the sun loses its power and the morning mist is slow to clear.

Once rain has fallen on the straw behind the combine there is little opportunity for it to dry out and be baled so that the ground can be prepared for the next crop. The dairy farmers in the heavy vales to the west of us have to buy all their straw from the arable farms and it is going to be very difficult and expensive for them to obtain dry straw this year.

I mentioned in June that we had plans to pump river water to the cows. When Sidfords sank the big concrete tubes into the meadow next to the river bank in August, we came across a copious spring that issues from under the farmhouse. I presume it was responsible for the house being built over it hundreds of years ago. As a result, the cows are drinking the spring water which flows through the tubes into the river. If the spring fails in a dry year the river water will flow back into the pumping chamber. The cost was considerable although we saved money by feeding all the electrical cables and pipes through existing drains. We hope it will pay for itself within two years so you will no longer have to put up with my whingeing about the enormous annual cost of the cows' water from the mains.

We are subject to world prices for food and one of the biggest consumers is China, which has doubled its wealth since 2001. Beef consumption there has risen by 75 per cent and dairy products by 400 per cent in the last decade, but China is self-sufficient in everything except soybeans. It now imports almost half of the world's production of this source of protein, which we also buy in bulk to mix with our own wheat and barley to feed to the dairy cows. It impacts on our grain markets as an area the size of all the UK's arable acreage is needed to satisfy the Chinese demand for soybeans. Now they are going all out to develop a variety that will grow in China. It is only about 25 years since we were first able to grow maize here successfully, so no doubt they will succeed.

I do hope to be able to give you better news next month.

December 2008

Many people driving down the road from Wardour have remarked on the redness of one of the apple trees on our lawn which has been covered with fruit. Unfortunately they are cookers, of which there is a glut this year. Even the ancient cider apple trees in the orchard have produced enormous crops which have tried the old branches, several of which have split. I fear that these veterans, which may be a hundred years old, are gradually decaying from inside.

It is fifty years since the mobile cider press arrived and I, the farm pupil, helped to scoop up every apple to be crushed. It was said that a better taste was produced by including all the rotten fallers and some bedding straw, and even dead rats were welcomed to aid fermentation. The golden liquid was kept on the farm in barrels for the following summer's harvest.

The very rough cider was decanted into jugs to be put in the corn fields where the reaper and binder machines were at work. Those engaged in the arduous task of 'hiling' the sheaves into triangles of six could slake their thirst and anaesthetise the pain in their arms from thistles by gulping a half pint at every revolution of the field. Three weeks later the sheaves would be lifted by hand onto wagons and then built into ricks to await the arrival of the threshing machine in the winter. At all stages the cider came out to raise the spirits of those engaged in the long back-breaking slog which was harvest before the combine arrived.

This year the autumn colours of the leaves were beautiful. We are filling up the spaces in the orchard with trees from our old friends, Landford Trees. The latest is a spindle. It is still sparse but the little leaves turned the deepest scarlet. They were not on the tree for long as the recent gales scattered them widely. They brightened the masses of leaves on the lawn rather like the red chillies scattered through the cheddar I bought at Salisbury market recently, called 'afterburner'. It certainly lived up to its name and made a memorable omelette one evening. There is a lot of pressure on British cheesemakers to encourage us to buy their products rather than imported cheeses. Much Cheddar and Wensleydale cheese now has added fruit to make it more tasty.

The price of heating oil is such that we have not turned on our central heating yet, though the Aga runs quietly on oil. It is so well insulated that it only takes the chill off the kitchen. We wear more sweaters and huddle round an open wood fire in the evening and have several small electric convectors which we can move round the house. We have been re-acquainted with porridge to get us off to a good start in the morning.

This has not much to do with farming but the need to reduce our carbon footprints must make us reappraise the economical use of our tractors and water heaters for the dairy.

It will be interesting for those who are farming Wallmead in fifty years' time to look back on our present practices which, by then, will seem so outdated.

March 2009

T he 1911 census has now been released early for public reference. The 1921 census will not be released until 2021. The 1931 census was destroyed by fire and none was taken in 1941. There is therefore going to be a long gap in the records.

In 1871 and 1881 Abdiel Combes senior and junior were the farmers at Wallmead. They were non-conformists, unusual on the staunchly Catholic Wardour estate, and were followed by James Street and his family in 1891 and 1901. Now we know that in 1911 Hugh George Burt was the 35-year-old farmer with his wife Katherine (30) and their children Katherine (3), Mark (2) and Monica (11 months). The Burts were and are still, mainly, RC. Catherine Martin (41), Hugh's widowed sister also lived here. They had nine rooms and no live-in servants. Agriculture had been through major upheavals during these 40 years since 1871 and there had been three tenancies at Wallmead.

This spring marks the Shallcross family's sixty years here as owners. Tom Doggrell was the last tenant before the farm was sold to us by the Arundells. Peter is the third generation of our family to be in charge. New blood is always needed or we get stuck in the past and try to make the old ways work. They usually don't.

The TV series *The Victorian Farm* has been giving us all great pleasure. It would be good if basket-making and many of the other crafts shown could be kept going but the farming demonstrated in the Shropshire time-capsule has been almost totally relegated to history, although shepherding has not changed much.

Many of the figures we put into our forward budgets are based on informed guesswork. The milk-price has been rising steadily and last month was 28p a litre so we were coming out of a loss-making trough and back to the amount we were getting eight years ago. Bang! The price is going down by 1.75p in February and may continue to slide. If we stay with dairying we have to increase the herd yet again up towards of two hundred cows. We started with forty Shorthorns in 1949 and bought a seriously dangerous Dutch Friesian bull, called Swart Lodkees, to increase the milking potential of the heifer calves.

More cows mean a longer milking time so we have decided to increase the number of units in the parlour from eight to ten a side. We had allowed for this possibility in designing the length of the milking pit, but the installation will cost about £12,000.

The lack of price security has already led to a reduction of nearly fifty per cent in the national pig herd. Sheep numbers are also on the way down and we have to import milk, mainly from the Emerald Isle.

It is gratifying that shoppers are now looking for local produce and the red tractor logo. This seems to be the only guarantee that 'British' means food produced in the UK rather than imported thousands of miles and processed here. This is a development that Wallmead's earlier tenants – the Combes, Streets and Burts – could probably not have dreamt of, although Woolworths had appeared in 1908. How many years is it since we were introduced to the forerunner of the supermarket? The local example at Crockerton was an emporium called Normans where the trolleys went crab-wise and the goods were stacked on the floor. Packets often burst and overflowed into the narrow concrete aisles. Ted Woods, our tractor driver, could proudly boast in The Crown that his ancient Ford Prefect had managed to return to Tisbury over Lords Hill, its little boot full of cheap food.

August 2009

People working with animals or enjoying the countryside are subject to health hazards from the diseases that animals, domesticated and wild, may carry. Tuberculosis is a disease which used to be caught in this country from drinking infected cows' milk. All cows are now tested regularly and any reactors promptly withdrawn from the herd. As far as I know, TB from milk is no longer a threat here but you will have read of the hot spots of cattle being infected in the West Country, not so far from us, which is ascribed by many scientists to infected badgers spreading the disease to livestock, even including alpacas. A trial programme of immunising badgers is about to begin.

Leptospirosis is a potentially serious bacterial infection, which is known as Weil's disease when spread by rats' urine; it can be contacted from cattle urine. It can wreak havoc in a dairy herd, killing many calves. The cattle can be vaccinated against it but there is no vaccine for humans, who have to be treated early with antibiotics. Both forms can be fatal to humans. We employ a rodent controller who tries to destroy the rat population in the farm buildings but there are always some around and they live in the fields in the summer.

A similar disease is Lyme disease, *Borrelia burgdorferi*, spread by ticks which live in long grass and rough vegetation, such as bracken, where part of their life cycle may be as passengers on deer. There were 813 recorded human cases in the UK in 2008, and the numbers are increasing each year with many more thought to be unreported; pets can be infected too. It was named after a village in Connecticut called Old Lyme, where it was identified in 1975 though it is worldwide. Not all ticks, which often attach themselves to dogs and other animals, carry the disease. I went to a recent Royal Forestry Society meeting at Tollard Royal on a very hot day, wearing shorts. The forester gave us a warning about ticks but said that, although there were many deer on the estate, no cases of Lyme had been notified.

Unfortunately some of the Tisbury ticks are infected as my ten-year-old grandson Billy experienced recently. The tell-tale round red rash was noticed and, although diagnosis was within three weeks of the tick bite, a long course of antibiotics was needed and recovery is expected to take two to three months. His loss of energy is very apparent. His mother Jane organised a meeting at St Johns School in July to bring the risks to public attention so people know that the key points are to remove ticks properly and promptly and to get treatment quickly if they get any of the initial symptoms.

After a country walk it is important to check yourself and children for ticks – especially between May and August (the ticks' most active times of year). All the folds in the body should be checked and any ticks removed carefully. You need to remove them quickly because they normally do not cause infection unless they are attached to the skin for more than 12 hours. The main point to remember when removing ticks is to get all the tick out without squeezing their bodies. This can be achieved using fine pointed tweezers or by using tick removers or lassos (available from lymediseaseaction.org.uk).

Some say you can kill them by applying Vaseline or even gin but researchers have reported that these methods cause the ticks to regurgitate, and may increase the chance of becoming infected.

It is not recommended to take antibiotics after being bitten by a tick, but if between three and thirty days later you get any of the following symptoms, see your doctor urgently: a circular red rash with a pale interior around the rash site (not seen in all cases), tiredness, joint aches, headaches, intermittent fever. If Lyme disease is treated early then it is usually very effective, but if treatment is delayed then there can be long-term health consequences.

October 2009

I n the five weeks since I wrote the September article all the harvest has been completed locally. Fortunately there was only one rainy spell in early September so the grain came off the combines at a low moisture content and little drying was needed. This was just as well because the prices are still at rock bottom, especially for barley. A much larger area was grown this year as the input costs are lower than for wheat.

Prices for cattle and sheep have soared. Even some ancient and much-loved cows made over £300 each this month. The young sheep we are buying this year to boost our 600 breeding ewes are likely to cost nearly £100 each but the first May-born lambs, only three months old, fetched £55 each. Our heavy clay land benefits from being grazed by sheep, called 'the golden hoof' by our forebears. However, it is rather wet for them in the winter and this makes problems for their feet. Last year we took on additional land near Ansty but the fencing was poor and they wandered off into the woods.

This year the flock will be grazing chalk downland near Burcombe farmed by the Combes family, whose forebears rented Wallmead from the Wardour estate in the late 19th century. Times were hard and some Combes were then in the Tisbury workhouse on Union Hill. They have thrived since, currently farming at Baverstock and Fovant as well, and the Alice Combes Trust helps our local needy in the present day.

Renewable energy still comes up in the farming press. We farmers would all like to make some income from wind turbines but lobbies are strongly against, at least 'not in my parish'. On the way to Lyme Regis I stopped to show my companion arguably the most beautifully sited church burial ground in the south-west at Marshwood, 650 feet above Charmouth. I was already impressed that the adjacent village school has adapted the church as a classroom but with a service still taking place there every Sunday. It earned even more marks in my book as its own wind turbine was turning furiously but completely silently in the playground. It is sited on a wind-catching ridge, no doubt putting energy into the grid and powering the church organ, with free heat or cooling for the school and church all the year round. In passing, I would point out that the Marshwood Vale was desecrated by miles of enormous electricity pylons several decades ago, but these do not seem to attract the fury of the lobbyists as do wind turbines which are a partial substitute to power stations.

Denmark is small in acres but big in pigs so there is a thriving research programme in designing anaerobic digestion plants to convert pig slurry into fertiliser having already used the process to generate power. Now here's a holiday for you with a difference: a 36-hour guided coach tour of plants in Germany and Belgium, cost £210. I think I will give it a miss this time, partly on the grounds that coaches seem to be designed for the transport of midgets.

In any case you need a lot of pigs on one site and deep pockets. A project near Truro in Cornwall has 750 sows, access to a lot of factory food waste, and a budget of £4 million. When it is up and humming we could book the Tisbus to have a look.

Local people,

past and present

Archibald Beckett and Robert Smythson

T he names of the builders who constructed the splendid old listed buildings in our area are largely forgotten. Some architects' names are recorded, however, such as Robert Smythson. He was a master mason and has been called the first English architect. He was building Longleat when Sir Matthew Arundell, who had bought the Wardour estate in 1570, engaged him to remodel parts of the old castle. Much of Smythson's stonework is still visible following its partial destruction in the Civil War 70 years later. I see that the magnificent Arundell coat of arms over the front door has been restored recently, having been concealed for many years.

It was surely coincidental that the acclaimed architects Peter and Alison Smithson bought a ruin at Upper Lawn from us in the 1960s and converted it into a Japanese-style house, now listed! This was of interest to the Hill family who lived in the adjacent farmhouse and overlooked the Smithsons' glass-sided, uncurtained bedrooms.

The first recorded builder of note in Tisbury itself was Archibald Beckett whose name and the date, 1885, are carved on the front of the Old Brewery which he rebuilt. More importantly Beckett laid out the whole of the High Street below the Benett Arms, which he also built. His name is remembered in Beckett Street. At the time he was living in Hindon with his wife and four children, having been born in Wilton in 1842. He described himself in the census as a plumber, brewer and maltster. He was born just as the railways connected London with Tisbury and enabled building materials to be moved cheaply round the country for the first time.

He was headhunted in 1888 by Boscombe, a new town which needed some important buildings to rival its neighbour, Bournemouth, hence its own pier. Beckett was commissioned to build, over the next eight years, Boscombe's Royal Arcade, the Salisbury Hotel and the town centre of shops and offices, now pedestrianised. His *pièce de resistance* was the Grand Theatre, a vast building opened in 1895. Its function and name has changed several times since and it is now undergoing major refurbishment to its former glory.

We now have a variety of local builders, but as Roy McGrath is in his nineties it is good to trace the origins of the firm he founded. Coming from Easterton near Devizes, where his father trained him as a bricklayer, he saw an advert for a live-in job working for Mrs Corry at Hill Street Farm as he came out of the RAF. He and his family moved five times locally, including living in a caravan at Hindon. He built his first house in Stop Street in 1950 and sold it to fund the next one; he never took out a loan. It was nearly ten years before he could afford to live in his own house in Church Street. His first development was to build the bungalows in Oddford Vale, a swampy site which he bought for £100. He sold them for just under £3,000 each. He still lives in one of them.

Michael has been running the firm of W.R. McGrath and Son for many years, assisted by several long-term employees who have worked for him since they left school. Gordon Culley, his office manager, has been with the firm for fifty years. They have built dozens of new houses, including Church Street Close, and repaired and extended hundreds more.

Roy helped with the estimating until well into his seventies but now, due to failing eyesight, he has had to give up his splendid painting of local scenes. He used to play a variety of wind instruments in local dance bands conducted by Reg Dicker and Billy Gold, whose evenings in the Victoria Hall helped many local romances to flourish.

August 2007

The Chilmark Dump

The Portland stone outcropping naturally in the Chilmark ravine, north of Ham Cross Farm, was very convenient for early generations of stone masons to extract. Deep horizontal mines then had to be quarried into the western hillside to follow the best seams underground. The firm of T.T. Gething started mining stone there in 1907 and was still there in 1936.

For security purposes, Ordnance Survey maps published for the following forty years showed the land as it was when, in 1937, the valley and mines were bought by the War Department for the storage of munitions. No. 11 Maintenance Unit, Chilmark came into being. Its motto was a bee and the words 'Mea Te Nocet', I sting you. The unit closed in 1995 and the board from the officers' mess recording the names of the 19 commanding officers hangs in the vestry at Chilmark church. Battle of Britain Sunday is celebrated there each year.

The history of 'Chilmark Dump', as it was known locally, should be written, as dozens of local people worked there. They have many memories to record. I will return to those 58 years another time, but this month I confine myself to a few paragraphs about the use of the site over the last ten years.

Decontaminating the heavily polluted and dangerous areas took many years and is still not completed. By 2003, £1.8 million had been spent on the clear-up.

Chilmark stone is quarried to the east of the road by Wessex Dimensional Stone. They still use part of the extensive narrow gauge railway system which moved munitions round the Dump. The bombs and shells were brought in by train from Dinton, where there were extensive sidings and storage facilities, via the single railtrack which still runs alongside the main line used by our trains and trans-shipped in the sidings near the engine shed. Some of the little 0-4-0 diesel locos are still active on preserved lines: *Chilmark*, built in 1940, is on the Bala Lake railway and *Jack* is on the Hollycombe Quarry railway in Hampshire. A commercial video was made of the last days of activity on the Chilmark railway combined with film of the Marchwood military railway on Southampton water.

ISSEE, the UK Centre for Homeland Security, now operates over 55 acres. It continues the expertise of training in explosives education and is directed by bomb disposal experts.

The southern tip of the long site was earmarked for one of the seven purpose-built Regional Government Headquarters to be used if H bombs fell on England. Construction was delayed until 1985; the Berlin Wall came down soon after it was completed and it was therefore redundant. It was sold soon afterwards. Plans can be seen on a website. A total of 150 office workers could be housed there, sealed off from nuclear fallout, with provisions for thirty days and 48,000 litres of diesel stored to provide power. Gloucestershire, Avon, Somerset, Dorset and Wiltshire would have been governed from Chilmark. A BBC studio was included. The ladies' loo, but not the gents', was fitted with a gas detector! Volunteers were sought from Local Authority staff to man the bunker but few were enthusiastic. It is now said to be used for the back-up of computer data and is unmanned.

In 2017, it was revealed that the bunker was being used as an illegal cannabis factory!

September 2008

Alfie Underwood – Electrician

Alfie Underwood was born in 1916 and lived at Newtown where he worked as an apprentice electrician on the Pythouse estate. When war broke out in 1939, he volunteered and spent seven years in the RAF. He came out as a corporal and engineer and started the first electrical business in Tisbury in a little lean-to close to the Overhouse Laundry.

The next-door business was the Tisbury Printing Works which was started by Peter Fulford and Cecil Jeanes. It was a thriving concern and they later moved it to the former British Restaurant in Rollestone Street, Salisbury. One of the employees was Doreen, who married Alfie in 1947. They later took over Disney's hairdressers shop in the High Street, and Underwoods is still the name over the door. Alfie's first partner was John Penny, who looked after the shop and later opened his own further up the hill.

While Tisbury's initial current was generated by an Armstead turbine in the River Nadder at Mill Farm (it may still be there), few people in the outlying areas had electricity; they relied on oil lamps and batteries, called accumulators, to power their radios. These were brought to the shop to be charged. When we came to Wallmead in 1949, mains electricity was about to arrive but for months we used petrol engines to work the vacuum pump to milk the cows.

Most of Alfie's outside contracting work was local and he was involved in the expansion of Parmiters. The estates at Fonthill, Pythouse and Hatch kept him busy. He trained a long succession of apprentices including Dennis Culley and Terry Ingram who both worked for Underwoods for over fifty years. Others moved away and started their own businesses.

Alfie was very involved in the community. He was governor of Dunworth School and chairman of the Victoria Hall Committee. He treasured articles of local interest and was keen to start a museum where they could be preserved. I think he would be gratified to know that a copy of this book will be kept in the archives of the village.

Sadly Alfie died in 1973 aged only 57. His widow Doreen carried on the business for more than a year with Dennis's help and then sold it to John Lewis and his family. She remarried and now lives at Westward Ho!

Alfie would have seen the original lead and rubber cabling replaced by plastic. I am told that plastic cabling should last for thirty years but a five-yearly wiring test is advisable. Underwoods now run four vans with the distinctive red paint-job. If I require a major item of electrical equipment I use the internet to compare models and prices or even visit some of the big stores in Salisbury. However, I then go to Underwoods to see if they will be competitive – they often are – and then get them to supply and install. Apart from supporting a local business and their employees, it is much easier to raise a problem with them than with a faceless national company who have tried to sell you a lengthy and expensive guarantee.

October 2010

Water meadows – Cyrus Combes

U ntil a hundred years ago, farms bordering rivers in much of the Avon catchment area from Christchurch to Salisbury and along the tributaries had the advantage of being able to flood their water meadows all through the year to stimulate the growth of grass for cattle and sometimes sheep. This was possible because engineers, some of them Dutch, had built a series of weirs and channels to very careful levels in order that the water of the various rivers and streams could be dammed and then made to overflow their banks. These systems had been kept at a high state of efficiency, some for several hundred years, until the beginning of the 20th century when the advent of artificial fertilisers and the high cost of maintenance meant that most of them became disused. Below each weir the water courses were divided into 'carriers', which took the water from the river and spread it at high level onto the land, and 'drawings' which collected it at low level to return it again to the mainstream. These carriers and drawings had to be kept at their proper level, slope and taper, and there was an old saying that 'the water should come on at a trot and go out at a gallop'.

In 1871, a Cyrus Combes set out the annual programme (starting each October), for drowning the Nadder meadows of Bridzor – he spelt it Birdsor – Hazeldon and Wallmead Farms, all in the parish of Wardour, which shared a single system. There had to be complete cooperation between the three farmers so that each would have several days of water before the next farm could be irrigated. Cyrus referred in his instructions to each farm having a 'pane' of land. I am not aware of this word being used in the context of land any more, although of course we have window panes and panes of stamps, a term known to philatelists. The times of watering were almost invariably known as 'stems', and 'lugg' was used as a linear measurement equalling a pole or perch. These words virtually disappeared at decimalisation, though they sometimes survive in measuring allotments.

I can just remember seeing the last working meadows being drowned at Britford in 1948. It was exciting to watch the water advancing along the carriers and being diverted over the grass by the 'drowner' using his spade to guide it with turfs.

From the 1871 census we know that Abdiel Combes was the tenant farmer at Wallmead and Elizabeth Gurd was the tenant at Hazeldon. Cyrus Combes and Abdiel were cousins. Cyrus was then aged 43 and Abdiel 40. Cyrus was living at Pool Lane, Wardour (where was that?), and had two servants in the house. The amazing statistic in the census form is that as a civil engineer and land surveyor he employed 95 men! He prospered and later on he lived in Prospect House along the Hindon Lane, one of the most imposing older houses in Tisbury.

The question arises as to how 95 'surveyors' – perhaps some were drowners – could find a living in the area. At that time the railway was well established and there was an enormous amount of building work going on. Tisbury High Street and the Brewery were being laid out by Archibald Beckett, most of the farm houses were being extended and some built from new. William Wyndham had built Phillips house and several farmsteads at Dinton and Chicksgrove. The new workhouse was being built and new roads constructed. All the drawing work would have been done by hand and Cyrus's team must have been in great demand.

When we came to Wallmead in 1949 there were still traces of the old water meadow system but it had not been in use for fifty years. The hatches at Bridzor were no more, so the water could not be penned back in order to start up the system; the three farms were now in private ownership although all had formerly been part of the Wardour Estate. So the water meadows were gradually levelled, but when the river overflows after storms there are some traces of the old system in the grass and stonework is evident in places.

November 2010

The Farmer's Boy

I have two photographs taken at the end of our first harvest in 1949 showing the harvesting team at Wallmead. There are nine men; in one photograph the men have all taken their flat caps off, something they had probably never ever done before outside a house. In the centre of each photograph is our second milker Jackie Ingram wearing gumboots, which denote his trade and may have been kinder to his corns than the leather boots worn by the rest. He is seated on a child's chair, about to pour himself a mug of rough cider out of a large enamel jug.

On the edge of each group stands the Sergeant Major-like figure of my father's first farm foreman, Bill Cornick, a short burly man who lived with his large family at Haygrove on the top of the hill above the farm. At that time there was no road to his cottage, no electricity and only a trickle of water. His trousers are tied with string below the knees and are held up by his braces and a stout leather belt. We were told that the leather belt was very useful in keeping order among his children.

At the back of the group is my father looking rather modest and proud. He would have been aged 42 and had just fulfilled his lifelong ambition of seeing his own first harvest completed. The rest of the men are a mixture of the regular hands such as Ted Woods and Ted Rixon, together with our dairyman Fred Rogers and several men who had been drafted in for the harvest, some of whom worked on the railway.

Wilf Rasen, the carter, is missing from the photograph. He was a shy man who still kept his singsong southern Welsh accent and looked after the two carthorses. He was probably putting them back in their stable after a hard day's work and I have a picture of one of them in full harness drinking from the trough in the yard. The cows were then all Shorthorns still with horns.

The rough cider is significant because it acted like a local anaesthetic on our tired and scratched feet and arms and so enabled the men, later joined by me, to carry out the very long and arduous work of bringing in the harvest by hand. This was before the days of combines. A small Fordson tractor pulled a reaper and binder. The sheaves all had to be propped up in rows of hiles, our local name for stooks, for up to three weeks before they could be taken to the ricks which Ted Woods would later thatch.

The next picture I have of our farm labour force was taken on my 21st birthday party in 1958 when my mother organised a slap-up meal for everybody at the Victoria Hall. By this time, Bill Hill had joined us with his family as we were then keeping pigs, and the farm manager was Joe Denham. The guest of honour was the vet, Bill Blanshard, and there are about thirty people present including the men's other halves, where they had them. The men were wearing their teeth for the occasion and seemed to be rather under the thumb of the ladies. Apart from my sister Ros and I and our mother Daisy who is now 98, everyone else in both photographs will have died some years ago.

Many town people still apply a farmer's boy image to those who work on the land. Cyril Legg was probably one of the last real farmer's boys. A keen smoker, he was just 67 years old when he died recently. He had retired from work on Tony Green's farm at Ansty a few years ago and moved to Tisbury. He was a familiar figure walking from his home in the Quarry down to do his shopping, always wearing immaculate green gumboots and the inevitable flat cap. It was only when his sister Joyce wrote to me from Northern Ireland that I realised that he loved historical novels and was a keen stamp collector. He was not an easy man to converse with, though he frequented the local pubs, and to most people he was just a nodding acquaintance. In fact, apart from about six members of his family, Philip Skinner and me together with Tony Green, nobody else came to his service at the crematorium.

Cyril never drove a car although he drove a tractor on the farm and at one time owned a 50cc motorcycle. When he turned right he could not let go with his right hand so he somehow managed to indicate right with his left hand across his body. On one of the rare occasions he left Tisbury he went in convoy to the speedway at Poole. On the way back he came to the unusual (for him) sight of a roundabout, and seeing his friends accelerating away to the left promptly took the shortcut anticlockwise to catch up with them. As we get older many of us are likely to be remembered as characters ourselves but Cyril was certainly one. The last farmer's boy in our community.

May 2011

My father, Jack Shallcross

I dris Kirby photographed my father Jack in the farmyard at Wallmead in the late 1970s. His picture looks at me now. He looks like me but rather older, except he was younger! He wears his trademark white moustache and some people called him the Colonel, though he never wore uniform after leaving his public school, Wellington.

He was born at the Rectory, East Harptree in the Mendips, the only child of elderly parents. His father, the rector of the Harptrees, died when Jack was 12. His best friends, later my godfathers, were a solicitor from Henley-in-Arden and a wool stapler from Oxfordshire. Between them they arranged for my father to spend his long school holidays on farms in the Midlands. He thought he would follow his father into the church but for some reason, thought to be slightly scandalous, was asked to leave Oxford. He then pursued a career in agriculture at Reading University which, although he wanted to farm, led to him becoming a fellow of the Institute of Chartered Auctioneers and also of the Royal Institution of Chartered Surveyors (RICS). He specialised in auctioning, arbitrating and valuing everything on a farm when a tenancy changed hands.

He became a partner in the old Salisbury firm of Rawlence & Squarey (R&S) before the war but was then called up to serve the Air Ministry in the West Country, buying land for airfields. He spent most of the war billeted in the Windwhistle Inn on the A30 between Crewkerne and Chard, with an office in a hut at Merriott. He was occasionally able to visit Ros and me and our mother Daisy at Alderbury during the war years.

When several farms on the Wardour Estate came up for sale soon after the end of the war my father, at the age of 41, bought Wallmead with its 240 acres and took over Miss Doggrell's Shorthorn dairy herd. He continued working for R&S, later called Humberts, for all his life and farmed Wallmead, and later Quarry Farm at Chicksgrove, with the help of a succession of managers, the last and longest serving of them being Philip Skinner.

My father never talked about his faith though he regularly attended evensong at St John's, Tisbury. My mother pointed out that he tended to turn his hearing aid off when I preached. I can't say I blame him: my take on the Christian faith has changed a lot in the last twenty years! He seemed pleased, however, when I was ordained in my forties though he'd been rather mystified by my long association with Buddhism. Having regard to his own father's profession I think he was pleasantly surprised that both Philip Skinner and I were ordained and running the farm before he died. He was only a year older than I am now, and Peter was coming along to succeed as the first hands-on Shallcross farmer in three generations.

I followed in his professional footsteps, joining R&S in the Sherborne office after Seale Hayne Agricultural College and an undistinguished national service in the Royal Signals, mainly in Bavaria. I then moved to the Southampton office where I met Jenny; then to Salisbury to join my father until he retired. In all I completed fifty years with the firm. I've always seen some connection between auctioneering and preaching. It is a question of trying to whip up some reaction from the company attending even if, as in church, they sometimes hide behind pillars.

My father loved a pint of bitter and indeed more than one at lunchtime or especially when playing skittles. He was a much respected agricultural arbitrator but as he got older he became, like me, a little deaf. I frequently acted as his clerk and when the arbitration continued after lunch he seemed to nod a little. I kept all the notes and ended up playing a major role in the decision-making. This stood me in good stead when I was appointed onto the RICS panel as an arbitrator myself, but I hope I just managed to stop before hearing loss got the better of me.

The partners of R&S all had to all take a medical examination for insurance purposes in the 1970s and my father, who never visited a doctor normally, submitted to the examination. The doctor found that he had a heart problem and prescribed medication which probably kept him alive for an extra ten years until he died in his sleep at home in the bungalow which he had bought a year or so before. Jenny and I with our five children came back to the farm where I had been in partnership with him for many years. We were similar characters and when I became a farming partner with him I kept clear of all decision-making. After he'd moved out of the farm he too distanced himself for any change that I was proposing for the future.

It is now thirty years since we moved back to the farm and Humberts, though now resurrected as a company called Chesterton Humberts, ceased to exist some years ago. One of my father's former partners Reggie Woolley set up a charitable fund for staff and partners called the Woolley Trust and recently, as the last Humberts chairman, I travelled to Coventry to the headquarters of the RICS to present to their pension fund, Lionheart, a jumbo cheque for £340,000. All former members of R&S are now treated as honorary members of the RICS if they fall on hard times. This seemed to me to be about the last act in wrapping up the old firm in which my father and I had worked for nearly a century between us.

December 2011

The Workhouse in our community

T wo hundred years ago the Wiltshire farm labourer had virtually no rights. He had lost his land under the enclosure laws and although he might have an allotment, he would not be able to make a living from it. You may remember from Thomas Hardy's *Mayor of Casterbridge*, set in the early 1800s, how farm labourers had to stand in line at the Michaelmas market to be chosen by a farmer to work for, and be housed by him for the next year. The unlucky ones and their families would become vagrants, having no house to go back to.

The first Poor Laws had been passed in about 1730 and each parish had a responsibility towards people within their boundaries who were unemployed, destitute and homeless. The funds had to be provided within the parish itself and local residents were required to foot the bill. You could imagine that no parish wanted vagrants to stay within their bounds for very long.

Gradually the larger parishes started to build what were called workhouses to provide roofs over heads. There was one at Semley and one at Tisbury, the latter since at least 1733. The parishes found it very difficult to cope with this problem individually and on 4 October 1830, the Tisbury Poor Law Union was founded as one of 17 covering all the Wiltshire parishes. The Union combined twenty parishes all feeding into the old Tisbury workhouse which stood on the site of the present brewery, just east of the parish church. There was a Board of Guardians made up of one person from each parish, with an extra one for Donhead St Mary which was very populous at that time. In 1831 census revealed that 9,763 people lived in the twenty parishes; the amount available for the relief of the poor was £8,250 a year, costing the inhabitants 17 shillings each (85p today).

An excellent website has been recently established by Peter Higginbotham with photographs by Peter Goodhugh. If you type in 'Tisbury Workhouse', you'll find it. There is a damning 1866 report giving details of the accommodation in the old workhouse but by that time the new workhouse on Union Hill, later known as Monmouth House, was being built and opened on 11 November 1868. The architect was Christopher Creeke, who also designed the workhouses at Chippenham and Blandford.

There is a link in the website to the 1881 census where the details of the 91 'inmates' and their places of birth can be found. Some were no doubt vagrants moving through, and housed for a short time. Several are described as imbeciles and one as deaf and dumb. People used to hide their meagre belongings in the roadside hedges before they were admitted and some local lads used to rifle through their bags and refill them with stones. There were 29 children resident aged four and over, described as scholars, and six children under four. The men and women were separated; there would be a tragic story behind each person there.

Eleven were retired farm labourers. I recognised over twenty surnames of families who still live in our community. The vagrants had to carry out work the next day to pay for their overnight stay and Walt Fry of Totterdale Farm is recorded in our archives as seeing as many as 38 men cracking stones on the road towards Mere in payment for their lodgings. If they skipped the allotted task and were caught by the constable, the penalty was usually seven days in prison. One cannot be sure whether the conditions were better in the prison or in the workhouse.

The workhouse also dispensed charity to the local population. Mont Abbott, an Oxfordshire farm labourer, recalls in his book *Lifting the Latch* how his mother, her husband being sick, trudged five miles to Chipping Norton to appeal for help from the Board of Guardians at the workhouse there. A local miller was the guardian on duty that day and awarded the mother of three one loaf of bread a week. When Mont's father was back at work again he determined that never again would his family be reduced to begging in this way. He subscribed to 'the Club', the Ancient Order of Foresters Friendly

Society. A small weekly subscription meant that if he was ever out of work again, the Club would give him a small income so the family would not starve.

I could go on but it was not until the Beveridge Report after the last war that the state started funding unemployment benefit at a reasonable rate. It was much later that an agricultural worker could claim security of tenure to remain in his cottage if he lost his job.

The Tisbury workhouse, 'the Union', was closed in 1935 and was empty until the war. Mr Warby had bought it and it was occupied temporarily by the military and then non-combatants: conscientious objectors and German Jews. I can remember following the scuttling Mr Warby along endless corridors to view the amazing second-hand furniture that he had collected from dockyards and elsewhere after the war. Eventually, the old buildings – which included a padded cell – were demolished in 1967. The houses of Castle Mount and High View Close were built on the site and part of the perimeter wall remains. The website contains many photographs of the building as demolition was starting.

July 2012

The Wyndhams of Dinton

In the 19th century two members of the extensive Wyndham family built separate farming estates in our area. In the first of two articles I want to talk about the estate of the Dinton Wyndhams, who originally bought property in that parish in 1690 from the South family. William Wyndham, who died in 1882, replaced the 17th-century Dinton House with the current mansion in 1815. It was renamed Phillips House when the estate was sold by his grandson in 1916 to Bertram Phillips, who subsequently gave it to the National Trust in 1943.

In the early 19th century William enlarged his Dinton estate in the Tisbury direction by the purchase or exchange of land with Lord Pembroke and some of the Wardour estate land possibly through marriage.

Having built Phillips House, William Wyndham then proceeded in similar style to construct three model farmsteads on the land he had acquired. Beautifully built in stone from the local Chilmark or Chicksgrove quarries these are Ley Farm, Teffont (1818), Ham Cross Farm, Sutton Mandeville (1830), and what is now called Quarry Farm at Upper Chicksgrove, then called Stoford (1833).

My father bought Quarry Farm in 1967. It was called Pophams Farm for many years and we still call one of the fields Poppins. I wonder whether the new farmstead was named in honour of Letitia Popham who an earlier William Wyndham had married in 1794. We recently sold Field Cottage which was dated 1706; perhaps it was the old pre-Wyndham farmhouse.

By 1883 the Dinton branch of the family owned nearly 6,000 acres of land in Wiltshire and 3,000 acres in Somerset. As well as building Phillips House and the three major farmsteads, William Wyndham also had the rectory built at Sutton Mandeville in 1832 and carried out major works on Sutton Mandeville church and other properties c.1862. Think of the army of men, including many skilled masons, who were given work for over thirty years. Some could have returned from the Napoleonic wars. William certainly left his mark on our Nadder Valley and all his buildings are now listed.

I've been lent the amazing 1875 Post Office directory for Hants Wilts and Dorset. William Wyndham was resident as lord of the manor at Dinton and was, like all the local gentry, a magistrate, and the Rev John Wyndham was rector of Sutton Mandeville. The Wyndham bailiff in Dinton was called David Darling, listed as 'Darling, David'.

I've also been lent the 1917 sale particulars of 2,000 acres of the Wyndham estate including Quarry Farm – 309 acres. The Wyndhams' estate had grown but then lasted for only a hundred years. Reading between the lines of the sale particulars, apart from other economic factors, it seems they just had too many children. William had seven and his son nine and, trying to be fair to each, this led to the break-up of the estate. William's grandson, the vendor, lived in Williton in Somerset, another part of their extensive empire.

They were a prolific family, though perhaps not unusually so at that time. George 1801–70, one of Letitia's sons, emigrated to Canada and then Australia, had 11 sons and two daughters, and was a pioneer in improving cattle and particularly vineyards.

Next month I will tell you about the Wyndhams of Clouds, East Knoyle, who included a cabinet minister, a spy and some rumours of scandal. The purchase of their short-lived estate was enabled by the problems of the Somerset and Dorset railway and was brought to a premature end by the 1914–18 war.

August 2012

The Wyndhams' Clouds Estate

Researching the history of the short 60-year story of the Wyndhams of East Knoyle is comparatively easy since Caroline Dakers published her fine book *Clouds, the Biography of a Country House* in 1993.

Percy Scawen Wyndham, 1835–1911, was the youngest surviving son of Col. George Wyndham who had been created first Baron Leconfield in 1859. He married Madeleine Campbell in 1860 and grew up surrounded by the priceless treasures of Petworth House. The family still own the Sussex estate although the house and park are National Trust property.

The Seymour family owned much of East Knoyle but in 1876 had to sell half their estate due to their disastrous investment in the Somerset and Dorset railway. Percy Wyndham bought it from them and immediately started planning a major country house for his own occupation. Work started on Clouds House in 1881; Percy occupied it in 1885 but it was burnt in 1889 and rebuilt. Percy lived in it until he died and was succeeded by his son George who was married to Sibell, Countess Grosvenor.

Sibell was a keen Anglo-Catholic. When electricity was first generated in an outbuilding, the basement lamp room became redundant and George and the estate carpenter, happily called William Mallett, transformed the room into a chapel for Sibell using Italian chestnut panelling. The family sat facing the altar and the servants to each side. Sibell was delighted and said that the new chapel reminded her of the forest of columns at Cordova and the underground church of St Francis at Assisi. George's tenure only lasted for three years; he died in 1913 aged 48, owning 3,000 acres including 15 farms and 87 cottages.

The First World War started and it was a disaster for the Wyndham family. Many of Madeleine's sons and grandsons died in the war and death duties crippled the family. One Wyndham who lived to a good age was her son Guy who was British military attaché at St Petersburg. He warned his Austrian counterpart in 1909 that British intelligence had found that an agent was sending top secret information about Austria's battle plans to the Russians. The Austrian reported back to his boss Alfred Redl in Vienna but Redl was the very spy himself! His enjoyment of dissipation at the Russians' expense was said to have cost the death of half a million of his countrymen in the 1914–18 war. When denounced by his successor, Redl committed suicide.

George was succeeded after his early death by his son Percy Jr, always called Perf, who only lived in Clouds for a year. He was an army officer who was immediately called up and died on the Western Front in September 1914. He left Clouds to his cousin Dick, the fourth and last Wyndham to own the estate. There had been three owners in four years and Dick, who never expected to own it, and could not afford to run it, was never very interested in the estate. Dick had been badly scarred by his experiences in the First World War. He was an artist and travelled extensively, partly in the Sudan where he loved the Dinka people and their drums. He bought two Dinka young lady models; one cost £4.

Dick Wyndham sold the Clouds estate in 1936. He had a drink problem and when he wanted to visit our area later he often stayed with his cousin David Tennant, who rented the manor house at Teffont Evias until it was requisitioned by the army in 1938. Dick lived dangerously and was killed in 1948 in Israel by a Jewish sniper.

Clouds seemed destined for demolition. It was resold for £3,300 in 1937; it had cost over £80,000 to build sixty years before. Eventually it was occupied from 1946 to 1964 by the charity now named The Children's Society, then caring for 'waifs and strays', unwanted children of which 534 passed through the house in twenty years, 42 being housed at a time. The majority left to be adopted. It was called the Beatrix Nursery and the children's nurses were in great demand as partners for the local young farmers at the hunt balls. Some live locally still.

Large Victorian country houses were being demolished after the war and the Seymours' East Knoyle house met its fate at about this time. However, Stephen Scammell bought the Clouds estate for the McLaren family and let it in 1965 as a school for fifty maladjusted boys. They were succeeded in 1983 by the Life Anew Trust who have occupied it very successfully as an alcohol and drug dependency treatment centre, being able at one time to accommodate 57 patients.

In the early 1960s, as a chartered surveyor I was asked to look around the house with a group of Tibetan monks who were wishing to establish a monastery there. They found it unsatisfactory but established Samye Ling in Eskdalemuir which has been run very successfully ever since. I was also involved in the dilapidation claim when the maladjusted boys left. They had not improved the fabric!

For the last 28 years I have visited Sibell's chapel nearly every Friday night to lead the Mustard Seed song group, initially with a Dinka drum which Alan Beale, our farmer friend from Ansty, had found in his attic.

Clouds House is humming with people and this June was the venue for the annual reunion of four hundred former patients. Caroline Dakers is sure that some of the patients could have been descendants of visitors to the house in the Wyndhams' time.

September 2012

Philip Skinner

Philip Skinner was born on 25 August 1930 in Bath. He had one brother Arthur, who became a scientist at Aldermaston, and who died about forty years ago. The parents were strict Plymouth Brethren and visitors, including Frances who was later his wife, had to eat separately from the family.

Philip went to Bath Grammar School and then had a scholarship to the Somerset Agricultural College at Cannington near Bridgwater; while he was there, he broke with the Brethren.

His first job was two years as an assistant manager at Hammoon near Blandford in Dorset. After a short spell at South Warnborough in Hampshire, he came back to Hammoon to work for Steve Hughes for whom my father was the land agent. Steve Hughes did not always make money available to pay the men so my father and Philip had to find ways of keeping the farm going. In the process they developed a respect for one another.

Philip met Frances at Wincanton races while she, a 21-year-old South Wales girl, was working in Sherborne. They had a whirlwind romance and after three months they were married in 1963 at Brynmaur in Wales. They first lived at Manston where Elizabeth was born.

On Boxing Day 1970 my father's farm manager Joe Denham suddenly died. Shortly afterwards my father phoned Philip to ask if he would consider taking over the post of farm manager at Wallmead Farm; he and his family duly moved into the manager's cottage on 17 February 1971.

My mother told Philip afterwards that my father had always asked prospective managers if they went to church and none of them ever did. At her suggestion my father had not asked the usual question to Philip – but he did, and never stopped!

The farm in those days was labour-intensive and Frances can remember preparing payslips for 14 people on the first week. Sadie Cooper our dairy lady had started a year earlier and together they were to work on the farm for well over twenty years.

Philip was a wonderful manager to my father for ten years and then to Jenny and me from 1981 for another 16 years until he retired at the age of 67. I, and others, could tell you so many stories about Philip's role in this village and his popularity in the churches and in the agricultural community, but space will not allow. He made many close friends, among them Bill Bown, Bernard Pike and Stan Harris.

When Philip retired he, Frances and Elizabeth moved to Ladydown House near the middle of Tisbury. Philip used to walk to the newsagents each day for his paper instead of taking the Land Rover as before. This walk, like all his forays into the village, involved stopping and talking to everyone he met, so the paper could be two hours late arriving at the house for breakfast. One of the main reasons that Ladydown House was purchased was because of its centralised position in the village and being within easy access for anyone to pop in for a chat, which many did.

Encouraged by Major General Keatinge who lived in Hindon Lane, Philip, after a lengthy training, supervised by a formidable nun, became a reader in the Anglican church. His sermons, delivered in his unmistakeable local accent and full of rural anecdotes, proved very popular wherever he preached, though he could get lost in the order of service!

Bishop David, being apprised of Philip's long and popular career as a reader, decided to ordain him at Michaelmas 1997. He was licensed to this benefice as a non-stipendiary priest, so Wallmead Farm had the unusual situation of the farmer and manager both being ordained.

On the day of his ordination in the cathedral there was a typical Philip incident when at 'the peace' he went walkabout to greet his friends and was swallowed up in the congregation. A verger was dispatched to locate him and return him to the platform where everyone was awaiting his arrival so they could continue the service.

Subsequently, Philip acted regularly as chaplain to the many visitors to the cathedral, enthralling people from all over the world with his reminiscences.

Philip died peacefully at home on 3 August 2012. We have lost a member of our community who knew practically everyone and was loved and admired by all who knew him. Someone, who is not a churchgoer, said that Philip lived the Christian life in a way that touched us all. He will be sadly missed but will live on in our hearts.

My mother

Thank you very much to everyone who was able to come to my mother Daisy's thanksgiving service at St John's on 11 January. She was 101 and I think 101 people came, an amazing turnout for a person of that age.

At the service I read out a letter which my sister Ros had found in our mother's possessions. It was from Fred Burt, Hugh's uncle, the then clerk to Tisbury parish council and dated 3 April 1968. His address was just West Hatch, Tisbury, Wilts, with no telephone number. Those were the days. He must have typed it just after an unusually short meeting. Daisy was the chairperson.

Dear Mrs Shallcross

Splendid, Wonderful, the best council meeting we have had for years.

What happened, did you mesmerise them? They were all like a lot of little children just starting school, even the General forgot he was a General ...

Yours sincerely

F J Burt

There is a picture of the members of the parish council in the early 1970s in the Tisbury Jubilee Book showing my mother in the chair and General Keatinge standing behind her with his bristling moustache. To my mother's left is a youthful Idris Kirby and he must now be the sole surviving member of the 16 people in the picture. Several people told me afterwards that they could not imagine my mother being so much in command of a serious meeting as she liked to interrupt any serious discussion by reciting one of her limericks, hopefully not too dirty, or repeating a story of doubtful veracity. Still, there must be lots we never knew about our parents.

Anyway we had lots of nostalgia in church, starting with the community singing of *My Bonnie Lies Over the Ocean, Pack Up Your Troubles in Your Old Kit Bag* and, of course, *Daisy, Daisy*.

When my parents came to Wallmead Farm in 1949 there was no electricity for a year or so. The house was lit by oil lamps and the milking machine powered by a petrol engine. My mother coped with these problems and was supported for about 25 years by our faithful live-in Irish cook etc, Maggie, an Irish spinster. She went regularly to mass but never understood a word as it was then in Latin. She used to bet on horses and seldom won. She was sure the priests would not approve and used to retreat to her bedroom if one called at the farm on his rounds of the faithful.

Maggie was great fun. She would shoot out her bottom set of false teeth to amaze visiting children. We used to push her round the drive in a wheelbarrow and her shrieks of 'Jesus, Mary and Holy St Anthony' could probably be heard in the presbytery in Wardour. She used to cook Sunday lunch and then go to Salisbury on the bus to see her Irish friends Peggy and Nora; it was great that they were able to come to the service. When the Sunday buses ceased to run, Maggie retired and lived for her last years in Laverstock.

On the farm the fields are saturated and springs are running as December was the wettest month for about twenty years (220 mm). The start of January has been wet too. However, the sheep are all outside as they are light on their feet and do not damage the grass. When the meadow flooded several times they just moved back to the strip of higher ground by the railway line. Last year's lambs are gradually being sold and soon we will be scanning the ewes to see how many lambs they are expecting to produce in May.

© Jane Alyson Smart

This is the quiet time of the year as we will not be able to do any fieldwork until the end of March at the earliest. All the berries in the hedges will now have fallen or been eaten by birds so we will be selectively hedge trimming along the roads and between some of the fields.

Local farms

and businesses

January 2006

Totterdale Farm

A s I approached Totterdale Farm, a sparrow-hawk flew out of the garden clutching a grey partridge almost as big as itself. The farm has been the centre of Graham Fry's shoot for many years and there is no doubt that the management of pheasants and partridges is also beneficial to most wildlife.

The Fry family have been farming in our area for centuries; before they rented Totterdale from the Wardour estate they farmed at Tuckingmill where other members of the family still live. Totterdale is a very old settlement and the core of the listed thatched farmhouse may be 11th century. It was part of the Tisbury manor of Shaftesbury Abbey, centred on the Tithe Barn at Place Farm. It was originally only about ninety acres in extent, owned by Souths and Barbers before becoming part of the Wardour Estate in 1760, two hundred years after the first Lord Arundell was granted the original Wardour Castle and its surrounding villages. Walter and Joan Fry bought the farm with 183 acres as sitting tenants in 1946. Totterdale was then a small dairy farm. The land runs up to Wardour Woods with a heavy Gault clay subsoil and seventy acres of woods. The arable land is mainly between Jobbers Lane and Tisbury Row.

Next they bought Court Street Farm from Satterley in 1969 and when their only son Graham married Jackie Sladen of Dinton, she brought some good chalk arable farmland into the business. Today with their sons Matthew and Daniel, both married and proud parents, they are farming about a thousand acres. The dairy was moved to a purpose-built unit above Dinton in 1998 and expanded to 260 cows, but falling milk prices caused a radical change in policy and the cows were sold in 2003.

Only family labour is employed on the farm and the future is seen to lie in an ever growing measure of cooperation with neighbours to reduce overheads as prices for arable produce are still so low. The hope for better long-term prices is seen to lie in substituting renewable energy for finite reserves of oil and gas. The government has recently announced that initially five per cent of all petrol and diesel will be produced from biofuels such as oilseed rape and sugar beet.

About 3,500 tonnes of arable crops can now be stored at Totterdale, half is grown by the Frys and the rest comes from at least six neighbouring farms including our own. Matthew, the marketing member of the family, carries the responsibility of bettering the prices obtained by the local cooperative stores at Stonehenge and Henstridge. He starts with the benefit of lower haulage charges and proximity to the ports for exporting grain. Two hundred beef animals are fattened each year, housed during the winter at Dinton, but the profitability of beef is very poor at the moment and efficient corn production lies at the heart of the Frys' enterprise. Average yields are surprisingly good having regard to the quality of much of the land. One drawback is that the family combine can only be driven from Totterdale to Dinton via Semley, East Knoyle, Hindon and Chilmark – usually at 5.30am!

On my way down Jobbers Lane from my visit to the farm, I was brought to a halt by a buzzard in the middle of the road. It was eating the carcass of a road casualty, probably one of Graham Fry's pheasants, which was too large for it to lift over the hedges. After inspecting the stationary traffic, it flew with its prey over the cars to safety.

February 2006

John Edgley of Furzelease

T he unusual animals which catch the eye when driving near Tisbury Row are llamas sharing a field with some Aberdeen Angus (AA for short) beef cows and a bull. Curiosity got the better of me so I visited John Edgley of Furzelease Farm.

John is a chartered engineer and a member for thirty years of the Royal Aeronautical Society. A designer of aircraft, he bought the farm and 25 acres in 2000 and more recently acquired the former Mekang premises by the Jobber's Lane railway bridge for the re-launch of his business under the name of AeroElvira.

Elvira is the name of one of 36 pedigree AA cows which have been built up by John and Sue Poulton, a farmer's daughter from Hampshire. They will soon have the run of about 150 acres of land as John has expanded, buying seventy acres of Tony Green's farm at Ansty. It has been renamed Choulden Farm, reverting to its medieval name which means, appropriately, 'calves down'. He has also bought land in Swallowcliffe village from the Hinxman family; this is still being farmed by John and Lizzie Ridout. The Ridouts used to live at Furzelease and are soon moving from Donhead to Cornwall to rent a 260-acre Duchy farm where they will expand their organic livestock enterprise.

Elvira's name starts with an E as did those of all her female ancestors and her descendants too. This is an AA herd-book rule, as is the need to do a DNA test on every bull to prove their parentage. They all look just black to me but John assures me that each is a character and quite safe, unless you get between a cow and its calf, dog walkers note! His senior bull Pumpkin has a particularly charming face, at least in John's eyes.

John is not a hands-on farmer except in emergencies and is well served by two part-time assistants. So far the emphasis has been on building up the herd. Fortunately 80 per cent of the calves sired by Pumpkin have been female. When the herd is complete at about fifty cows, the bull calves will be more valuable. Two more bulls, Emulark, bought in, and Just Eric whom John has reared, are mating with Pumpkin's daughters and will hopefully produce at least 50 per cent males. Emulark needed another DNA test and did not object to being relieved of a tail hair for the purpose. Did not turn a hair?

John is convinced of the merits of organic farming and has been able to benefit from conversion grants which will be replaced by the new Organic Entry Level Stewardship Grants. So far only five steers have been sold; the AA reputation means that they find a ready local market. As with the other farmers I have visited, John sees the future in co-operation and hopes to join a small group of similarly motivated organic farmers to market their beef together.

So why llamas? The original male ('Guess My Weight' at the Swallowcliffe village fete) was bought as a pet and seemed lonely. Two females came along to keep him company and produce one little 'cria' a year each after an 11-month gestation. A pair of crias sell at ten months old for about £800. Their destiny is to be pets as, unlike alpacas and bison, they have no commercial value. Perhaps John should try reindeer as well; they are docile, easily led and command celebrity-size fees for towing Santa's sledge in shopping malls, though none has appeared on Big Brother yet! I may be over optimistic about the potential for reindeer; the two Swallowcliffe donkeys are still too unreliable to go into St Peter's Church on Palm Sunday, even after years of training.

David and Jane Collis

For a change I thought I would inspect the shop where we buy the most important part of our daily diet. So I visited David and Jane Collis whose little shop provides us all the year round with the five portions of fruit and veg that our bodies need each day to keep healthy.

While I was inspecting their wares a steady stream of appreciative customers came in. One lady said 'this is the most important shop in Tisbury' and I could see her point. David has run the business for 26 years. Until Christmas 2004 he got up at 4am each day to select his produce at Southampton market. You may remember his battered white van parked outside the shop making for interesting traffic conditions in the High Street. Now a wholesaler delivers his order daily from a similar market at Bristol. Quality is all important, each item must be perfect and the shelf life of much of the veg is very short, sometimes only a day or two. The Collisses and their staff have to work in cool conditions as nothing is chilled. Four degrees centigrade would be the ideal temperature but 10 to 15 is more normal. No office worker would stand that.

David sources his produce from the west of England wherever possible. The Vale of Evesham is the nearest large growing area: most of the roots go from there to Bristol, as do cooking apples. This keeps the dreaded food miles down. Potatoes come from Warminster, cauliflowers are grown in Devon and his eggs come from Dorset. When I interviewed him the early potatoes were sourced from Italy; soon the Egyptian crop would arrive followed by Jersey and then Cornish. David believes we, his customers, can still be discerning enough to wait for food in its season unlike those who expect the same fresh veg on the supermarket shelf all the year round. You will only be able to buy asparagus from him when the English crop is enjoying its brief season.

Tomatoes are a twelve-month requirement and they and the cucumbers were grown in Spain. Watercress is the most local crop being grown by the Hitchings family at Broadchalke; the mushrooms are from Whiteparish but Spain and Israel produce most of the more exotic winter fruit and veg such as avocados, celery, new carrots, lemons and sweet potatoes. Seville oranges were in their six-week season in January for marmalade making. Bananas have to come from the West Indies and the only African fruit I saw were table grapes from South Africa.

If we all ate our five portions a day we would all be healthier and David wouldn't have to throw so much away when he has a clear-out on Mondays. He was sadly contemplating a survey which said that people aged under 24 hardly ever cook veg and probably were never shown how. The average time for the preparation of a meal is now less than ten minutes.

I was most impressed by the care which David takes to present his produce so freshly and the skills he brings to his work. We all know that his reaction to his customers too is invigorating at times!

I didn't do a 'food miles' calculation on a typical basket-full of his fruit and veg but I read in the *Farmers Weekly* recently that they had worked them out on a Christmas lunch. A small shop in Devizes clocked up 163 miles, a farm shop in Yorkshire 453 miles and two major supermarkets 1,665 and 1,649 miles! The Devizes figure would have been less if they had not had to order the Christmas pudding from 104 miles away.

October 2006

Brewing in Tisbury

Before the days of mains water in pipes the inhabitants of our valley had to rely on wells or even streams. Often the water was polluted and people of all ages drank locally brewed ale which was safer. Nearly every pub brewed its own beer. In 1868, Mr Archibald Beckett of Hindon bought the old workhouse next to the church. The new workhouse had just been built on Union Hill. Mr Beckett turned the old one into a brewery and laid out the present High Street. The brewery was destroyed by fire and Archibald's name is carved above the gateway of the new brewery which he rebuilt in 1885, naming it the Wiltshire Brewery. It continued to slake the thirst of beer drinkers in the area. It was owned by the Styring family and then by Eldridge and Pope of Dorchester, who closed it in 1914. In 1984, the Tisbury Local History Society produced a useful history of the building's subsequent many uses and Rex Sawyer tells the school children the story of the brewer's monkey that jumped into a vat and drowned.

There were gallant attempts to reuse the brewery for its original purpose between 1980 and 1983 by the Tisbury Brewery and then until 1989 by the Wiltshire Brewery (again). The 1980 revival happened when a Scots biochemist, Alastair Wallace, saw the potential of the building from the railway and bought it. His team included Tony Boyce who was the marketing man. John Hooper and Steve Jay worked for both companies. The first beers were called Tisbury Local, Tisbury Heavy and Old Grumble. One won Supreme Champion at Bristol in 1982. Later, Stonehenge and Old Devil appeared. Both brewing companies owned the South Western Hotel during their short lives. The Old Brewery has recently been converted into flats but the carved stone inscription has been restored by Eddie Closier, so Archibald Beckett lives on. Incidentally, one of the previous generation of Becketts was known to be so excitable that he had to be locked up by his family in Hindon during the Swing Riots in 1830. Local men were transported or hanged for rioting against the introduction of new agricultural machinery but he was saved.

More recently local small-scale breweries have been appearing. There is the Hidden Brewery at Dinton and this summer Alasdair and Charlotte Large, who live in Tisbury Row, have opened the Keystone Brewery in the old carpenters' workshop at Berwick St Leonard. Their mothers, keen real ale drinkers, have been acting as guinea pigs for the new brews. The Royal Oak at Swallowcliffe was honoured to sell the first barrel of the Large One. Fonthill Spring Water is the 'liquor' and malting barley will be specially grown next year on the Fonthill estate. Four beers are available kept in casks, painted with Alasdair's regimental colours. One priority is for light, low-alcohol beers with an eye to ladies' preferences, but the real ale enthusiast should be interested in the results.

Already the beers are available throughout the Nadder Valley and have been spotted as far away as the Isle of Wight and Manchester. The name Keystone was suggested by the wedge-shaped stone at the top of the Fonthill Archway; the masonry theme will be followed in the names of the other beers to follow: Bedrock and Cornerstone.

February 2007

The Art of Thatching

Leslie Parsons retired 15 years ago and one of his successors as local thatcher is Michael Read who lives and thatches at Chilmark. He mainly works in Ansty, Swallowcliffe, Teffont and Fonthill Gifford. Mike comes from a family of Winterslow thatchers but learnt his trade from Philip Dimmer, a Chalke Valley thatcher, and married his daughter Julie. He is related to most of the Wiltshire thatching families. Julie's uncle once disappeared through a rotten straw roof in Wilton, landed on the bed below and went back to his ladder via the front door. Thatchers seldom voluntarily look inside roof spaces. When the pole rafters collapse, as they frequently do, the dip in the roof is made up with more bundles of straw. It is usually only when a surveyor examines the roof space, as I used to do, that the problem is identified. Often there was no trap-door access so ignorance was bliss!

Combed wheat straw is used on average on six of the eight roof slopes which Mike tackles in a year; he uses water reed for the other two. Water reed can last for twice as long and does not need netting, but is frowned upon by the planners, although the difference in the finished product is hard to detect. Water reed is more expensive than straw. Les Parsons used to cut it at the salterns, the flooded meadows at Lymington.

Five thatchers from Norfolk brought their own water reed to re-thatch the Great Barn at Place Farm in 1971. It took them four months to remove the old thatch and replace it with 130,000 bundles weighing 270 tons. They said that the reed should last between 60 and 100 years. Now most water reed comes from Eastern Europe. During the foot-and-mouth crisis, thatchers were denied access to the woods so could not make their spars of split and twisted hazel to secure the bundles of thatch. Now spars can be bought cheaply from

Poland but must be used green, as they soon dry out and are then useless. Plastic spars are available and cheaper but Mike sticks to hazel.

The life of the straw on the weather side of a roof has only half the life of the other side – 20 years and 40 years – so only one slope, together with the ridge, needs to be recoated at one time. One side of a small roof can cost £5,000 to recoat these days. In the 1950s, £400 would thatch both sides.

The regular appearance of the ends of the straw is achieved by the use of a 'leggett'. The example which Mike showed me is made of grooved aluminium. It has to be struck hard at exactly the right angle against the butt ends to drive the straw tighter into the strings. Each thatcher carves his own wooden leggett-handle to suit his grip.

Thatchers can work in the rain, but not when the thatch is frozen. It is a tough life. Regulations now ensure that scaffolding is used for working higher than three metres from the ground so there is not the same risk of falling off a ladder. Very few farmers grow thatching straw and there is only one local combing machine based at Martin.

Using local thatchers ensures uniformity of style. Mike does not favour the ornate raised ridges that are now common. They weather much more quickly than traditional flat ones, but clients often want their roofs finished with a flourish.

Recently some local new houses have been thatched; there is one in Duck Street. Insurance premiums for thatched houses are much more expensive due to the risk of fire. Policies are issued subject to frequent electrical tests.

Recycling

We have only moved house twice. The first time, 42 years ago, our few bits of second-hand furniture were moved by Reg Maidment. Reg had previously driven lorries for his brother George, whose business A.G. Maidment had been a large employer in the area moving livestock and meat. Reg had got started by buying Mr Chivers' carrier's van in 1956 and when he moved us had just a single small lorry which bore his name. Now you can see that name, R.V. Maidment, on the cabs of six lorries. They each haul one of the 450 skips of assorted sizes holding from two to forty cubic yards of waste material which Reg's son Bob dumps in his large building on the A30 at Swallowcliffe. Five men work in and around the shed sorting the contents of the many skips which come in each day.

Until Bob moved to Swallowcliffe about 12 years ago all those skiploads, after minimal reclamation of hardcore and timber, would have been buried in a hole in the ground at Semley. This changed with the advent of land-fill tax and then, last year, a prohibition on the burial of any waste materials on farms without a licence and the banning of all burning of waste materials except hedge cuttings. It costs Bob £60 per ton to tip in an approved land-fill site; the nearest are all over an hour's drive from here, and haulage costs are high.

Bob realised that a large proportion of the waste collected in his skips could and should be recycled. His men extract from the tons of unwanted materials, metals, wood, cardboard and polythene. The remainder is screened and then crushed to separate soil from hardcore; a magnet removes any remaining metal. Of all the waste which is skipped in each day, 80 per cent is reclaimed for reuse and 20 per cent is tipped in the distant land-fill sites.

It is a struggle to get an economic price for the reclaimed material though every ton reclaimed avoids the dreaded land-fill tax. Most of the cost of this essential operation is paid by us for the use of the skips. Several government agencies are alert to the possible environmental problems of managing an operation of this scale and it is hard to comply with their complicated, and at times conflicting, regulations.

The building at Swallowcliffe is called the Western Works. This large shed with the adjoining Eastern Works was constructed by Wilf Stainer, probably in about 1948. They adjoined a hotel known as The Cribbage Hut, later The Lancers. At its peak 150 local men were employed in the two works reconditioning army vehicles. Terry Wheadon and Rodney Bowen worked there for a combined service of over seventy years. Fifty years ago I can remember convoys of battered desert camouflaged vehicles being unloaded at Tisbury station after the Suez debacle and being dragged up Jobbers Lane before returning for duty as good as new. The last contract before Mr Stainer died involved Army Air Corps fuel bowsers; by that time only seven men were left. He also bought hundreds of surplus vehicles at auction to rebuild and resell them, sometimes to Africa. It was recycling on an enormous scale.

Land-fill sites, like the Salisbury District Council one near Firs Road east of Salisbury, are full and closing. The contents of our dustbins end up in a pit at Calne! Some say the future lies in burning our rubbish, but recycling is the best way of avoiding waste. At present the resale value of most recycled materials hardly pays for the work of separating them out. It is up to us to do the initial separating and reduce the amount in our black bags to a minimum. It is possible we may be charged for their collection before long.

May 2007

Squalls Farm

S qualls Farm, which lies just within Tisbury parish on the Ansty border, was another of the Wardour estate farms that were sold about fifty years ago. The farmhouse was 17th century, low, stone and thatched. The land was mainly on the Gault clay. We had deep sympathy for Charlie Parsons, our neighbour there, who struggled to make a living out of the mud. Alan Parsons was brought up there and wisely decided not to follow in his father's boot steps.

Squalls estate now extends to about 400 acres, all in grass with woodland. The transformation began in 1971 when Ronald Saffron, who was reputed to have invented the first aerosol spray cap, bought the core of it. He extended the house and built a stable block using materials from Fonthill House. Mr Coombes was the next owner, who added more land. He sold in 1986 to the present owner, John McCarthy. John's story is a fascinating one. He was brought up in Lymington, failed the 11-plus and could not wait to leave school. Several of his uncles were joiners; he finished a five-year apprenticeship in joinery and carpentry when he was 21 and immediately went into business in 1961. He built his first house at 23.

In 1976 the government decided that we were living longer and needed retirement homes. John more or less created the concept of building retirement flats in the private sector with a house manager and a common room – a bit like Nadder Close, but where the residents each bought a long lease on a high-spec flat which they able to sell on. Eventually McCarthy and Stone (John's company) built over 40,000 such flats before John retired a few years ago. Since then the company has been sold for £1.1 billion. The first development was 32 flats on the site of the New Milton cinema. These were all sold before the roof went on! Later they covered the country from Falmouth to Scotland and even abroad. Peverell was set up by John to look after the residents; he no longer owns it but it is probably the biggest residential management company in the country.

One of John's many recreations is polo. You will have seen the once-immaculate ground which he created on the A30 above Ansty and where Prince Charles played for six years. Sadly a fall from his horse in 2000 put John in intensive care for a week and foreshortened his playing career. His sons' polo ponies are wintered there now. The Frys rent some of Squalls and the rest is used for the breeding of Dutch Warmblood show jumpers. Five people work on the estate.

John practises his skills in his workshop making furniture, doors and windows. The attention to detail is amazing and most of the oak is sourced from his own woods.

Two of his sons follow in his steps with their own retirement property company: Churchill. Their first job was the reconstruction of Spilsbury Farm Cottage; when I had auctioned it only the gable walls were standing. John's daughter, who lives in Belgium, is an international show jumper.

Squalls estate is a showplace with many unusual features lovingly designed and built by John. It is also an example of the use of land for equestrian purposes, providing local employment when farming wet marginal land no longer makes economic sense.

July 2007

Flushing in the community

When the Beales farmed South Farm, Ansty they had a very efficient pig unit close to the house. The family all worked with the pigs and were used to handling large quantities of manure which was spread on the surrounding arable land.

Pig prices go up and down in an unpredictable cycle and eventually Rob, soon followed by his sister Lydia, decided that the financial rewards did not justify the high pressure and smelly seven-days-a-week work they had engaged in since they had left school. Lydia moved to office work and Rob bought a lorry and went into the agricultural haulage business. Soon his father Alan suggested that emptying septic tanks might provide a better living.

Rob bought his first second-hand tanker in 1992 and soon realised that there was also a demand for portable toilets. He now owns 350 which are transported within a 40-mile radius of Ansty on four vehicles. The tanker fleet grew and he owns five of which four are on the road each day pumping out about 5,000 septic tanks a year.

There are said to be about 800,000 septic tanks in England and most need emptying annually. They hold between 600 and 800 gallons each and the partly treated effluent discharges into the ground, provided the soakaways work. Before septic tanks were invented there were cesspools. They are sealed tanks and still have to be used, and emptied frequently, in sensitive locations like Wiltshire Wildlife's Langford Lakes. In 1880 the city of Baltimore had so many overflowing cesspits that it was said to smell like 'a billion polecats'.

As there is no main sewerage in the Chalke Valley, Rob is well placed to service that area which is on his doorstep but powerful engines are needed to take his 3,000-gallon tanker lorries up Ansty Hollow. They only do about eight miles to the gallon and he charges a minimum of £113 per customer for up to one hour's pumping. No VAT is charged for emptying domestic tanks.

If he has emptied your tank, its capacity will be shown on his office database. Using this information, he can plan a route to collect a full tanker load. Each is emptied in one of eleven sewerage treatment works in the area. Rob employs ten people, more in the summer when the demand for mobile toilets increases.

Rob attends the big annual Pumper and Cleaner Expo at Nashville in the States where he is known as a PRO – Portable Restroom Operator! Here he keeps up to date with the latest developments. If you visit his website there are photographs of the line-up of his entire green lorry fleet and interior views of the latest improvement: trailer toilets complete with fresh flowers, a full stereo system and much more. All are tested by his competent staff before use. Now there's a holiday job...

His worst nightmare is a deluge at the Great Dorset Steam Fair or the Big Green Gathering where he may have 150 'restrooms' in action. Tractor-hauled trailers have to be used when the lorries can't move round the site.

What would we, who don't pay drainage rates, do without him? The days are long gone when the Chalke Valley growers paid their neighbours to fertilise their watercress beds by tipping their night-soil buckets in every morning.

November 2007

Flowers in the community

P eter took a day off milking our cows in September to go on a railway excursion from Warminster to Llandrindod Wells, the county town of Powys where he spent three hours and came home. What was L W like? 'It was a place with real shops.' I knew what he meant – just like Tisbury. Larger places have the predictable shop fronts of all the multiples and you have to explore side streets to find real ones, if the locals are fortunate and they have survived. How lucky we are with the variety of the shops in our High Street and the excellent service we get.

Ted Martin's flower shop bustles all day whether anyone is visibly shopping or not. Ted, who was a nurse for 25 years, employs eight people, some part-time. Fresh flowers are sent by courier van all over the country, competing with the smarter supermarkets; her website gives examples of her style of work and some of the events they have worked on. Flowers are supplied and arranged in private houses. Special events call for all sorts of themes and colour schemes, occasionally working with the local flower group for weddings. People visit from miles around.

Flowers come in from Holland nearly every day as they must be sold quickly. English suppliers would be appreciated but simply can't compete with the dependability and quality of the Dutch.

Ted found she had green fingers and started giving away flowers from her own garden before going on courses and starting in business. She celebrated five years in Tisbury last month, having moved a few doors uphill to her present shop three years ago.

She is pleased that many people like to buy flowers in season, white in the spring and ending with the rich autumn colours of the chrysanthemums. (Thank Microsoft for spell checker, though it could not manage Llandrindod Wells and suggested pewees for Powys in my first paragraph.) However, roses and lilies are in demand all the year round. Ted sells a book called *A Year in the Life of an English Country Flower Shop* by Sally Page. It will tell you all you want to know about what goes on, starting with a Chinese proverb: 'If you have two pennies spend one on bread and one on a flower.'

Sadie Flower is a very seasonal flower grower who, with her partner Mike, last year started planting two acres of the family farm at East Hatch with flowers. People can enjoy the freedom of a big flower garden and pick their own from June until the end of September. A bucket of flowers costs £5. There are beautiful colour pictures of the flowers on their website. Each year the plantings will diversify and permanent features will emerge. How lovely to be able to select sunflowers and choose a big bunch of sweet peas in favourite colours just a short distance from home!

Years ago I can remember keen ex-army officers starting to grow flowers as a business in the family walled garden at West Dean with a crumbling unheated greenhouse, neglected since the gardener was called up to fight Hitler. After anxious weeks the gladioli came into glorious bud just at the same time as everyone else's. They did not cover the cost of their transport to market. Only the brave enter this business and we hope that these local entrepreneurs will thrive. They will only continue to do so with our patronage.

April 2008

Pottery – Kate Good

O ur ancestors who lived on Salisbury Plain 4,000 years ago knew all about pottery. Clay was dug locally and the communities lit great bonfires to fire their everyday pots for storing food. Craftsmen fashioned beautifully decorated pots which the Beaker folk buried in their graves.

In 2,000 years' time, people may be finding shards stamped 'KG Tisbury' on the base. This would have been an example of the fine pottery which Kate Good has been making, first at Upper Lawn and then in the High Street, for over 25 years. I would not be surprised if the lights in the neighbouring shops flicker every month or so when Kate turns on her kiln; it uses 14kw of power to fire her pots up to a temperature of 1,260 degrees centigrade.

Kate's artistic imagination was awakened at the age of 16 by the sight of her first kick wheel. You can see an example of this back-breaking, foot-driven wheel at the back of her shop. Now it is only used for applying the glazing to the 'biscuit', the pots of still-porous clay, which have been shaped and heated to over 1,000 degrees; many of these are stacked along the back wall of the shop.

After studying art at school Kate embarked on a long training at several colleges finishing at the Central School for Arts and Crafts in London after which, with a few friends and a kick wheel, she embarked on a commercial venture selling their wares to smart London shops. Then it was Norfolk and family life with the first of her own kilns. Thirty-five years ago she came to Mere before moving nearer to Tisbury and making a name for herself.

Her clay comes from the potteries of Stoke-on-Trent and she mixes all her colours by hand apart from a rich terracotta which she buys in. As an ignorant non-artistic farmer, I brightened up at the mention of Stoke-on-Trent as I had visited one of the last of hundreds of traditional potteries which has been preserved as a museum. I even knew what a 'saggar' is and remembered how, in those high conical kilns, hundreds of pots used to be packed inside the pottery saggars and fired with coal in an atmosphere reeking with smoke, fumes and chemicals. The saggars could last 30 firings and their bases were made by boys called 'bottom knockers'. Look on the Potteries website and you will find a list of nearly 30 types of pottery made from nine different materials.

In Kate's showroom my eye was caught by the four decorative designs which she has evolved. The seagulls on a blue background have been available for twenty years. Marbling, each example quite different, has been in production for fifteen. I then decided that I really liked the grapevine pattern which started with a circular dish which Kate designed for the wedding of her son Duncan and Sarah on 4 July 1992. The background is a dreamy rather mystical blue. I am allowed to tell you that the leaves are cut out of lead flashing and removed with a magnet from the glazed pot using a drawing pin. I don't think you will find that on the internet! A first for *Focus* magazine.

Then, near the window, there is something really exciting. Dishes, each a masterpiece, bearing the hand-coloured imprints of real leaves, some from South Africa, but a common Nadder Valley buttercup leaf looks just as exotic. Right by the window glass is a lump of our very own unique fossilised Tisbury coral and lots of jewellery made from it in the village. I, who find a visit to the Clark's Shopping Village a foretaste of hell, enjoyed every minute of my time in Kate's shop.

Need I urge you again to support our local artists and businesses?

December 2009

The Fonthill Stud

P aul Leach took up his role as Manager or Head Groom at Fonthill last year and works with his partner Robyn and two other full-time staff. They manage the mares under their care on 80 acres of beautifully manicured post-and-rail-fenced grassland overlooking the lake and close to the cedar-fringed site of Alderman Beckford's great house, remembered now chiefly by the nearby Beckford Arms and approached through the Alderman's magnificent stone arch from Fonthill Bishop.

Paul was brought up with horses on a family farm in mid-Devon and was a national hunt jockey for 15 years. Thoroughbred colts and fillies are bred at Fonthill for flat racing. Thoroughbreds were bred from Arab horses about 200 years ago; now the oil-rich Arabs buy horses bred in Europe.

As a professional jockey Paul had 300 wins for the West Country trainers David Barons and Martin Pipe. He once came second in the Cheltenham Gold Cup, having arrived by helicopter from Exeter, and had one Grand National ride: unfortunately he parted company with his steed six jumps from home. Ten stone was the maximum permitted weight limit so he retired from competitive riding at 33 and became a trainer with 15 to 20 horses in his yard near Taunton, training them for both flat racing and the sticks; he clocked up 30 winners.

The stud at Fonthill, which is owned by Fonthill Farms, was founded in 1952 by John Morrison, MP for Salisbury from 1942 to 1964. He was the first Baron Margadale and his title comes from the family estate on the Isle of Islay, off the west coast of Scotland, famous for its many whisky distilleries. He was a prominent back-bench Conservative who predicted the rise of Margaret Thatcher.

Now his grandson Alastair, the third Lord Margadale, has taken over from his late father James and directs the breeding policy that has brought many successes to Fonthill. The excellent Fonthill estate website names some outstanding horses which have been born at Fonthill over the years; prominent among them is the mare Set Free, from whom three classic winners were bred in the 1970s. Her bloodline continues.

Stallions are not kept at Fonthill, only eight mares and foals and the family hunters. Ideally the mares should foal every year in the early spring so their foals can be sold as yearlings in their second summer. Some are retained and sent for training with Alastair's brother Hughie at West Ilsley; see his website too. As a horse's gestation period is 11 months, some smart timing is involved. Mare and foal cannot be separated at this early stage so they travel in a horsebox to a suitable stallion probably at Newmarket or Whitsbury, with a large fee involved, either for a stay of six-to-eight weeks or for a 24-hour visit, called a walk-in!

The Fonthill Stud is well known in the racing world, but operates quietly in the Park unnoticed by most of us passers-by. It contributes financially to our community in many ways. While the costs, not forgetting vet and insurances, are high, the potential rewards can be amazing in the highly specialist international world of flat racing.

February 2016

Butchers in Tisbury

When I was a boy in Tisbury, the butcher's shop was always in the premises now occupied by the deli. Paul Wishart was the butcher for many years, supported by several assistants. George Maidment's lorries used to come from the abattoir in Salisbury and sides of beef, whole pigs and lambs were carried across the pavement to be cut up into joints within the shop. For this purpose there was a large wooden block, very stained and worn. An armoury of sharp choppers and knives were used after much sharpening to cut up the meat to the required size in front of the customers. The striped aprons, still used in the trade, became blood-stained. Bones were taken away for dogs.

Not much else was sold apart from meat, and there were the usual special orders at Christmas for turkeys and other poultry.

On Sunday mornings my father and I would go to the Crown Inn. With Paul Wishart and Ben Gillingham the coalman, we would stand just inside the door and enjoy pre-lunch drinks. In those days everyone had a Sunday roast and we had to be back home by one. I can always remember that I used to drink a Gibbs Mew Special, brewed in Salisbury, in those days. The whole of the city centre used to enjoy the smell of brewing on the same day each week; dray horses used to take the barrels round the city pubs.

The authority on the history of butchers in Tisbury was Toby Baker, who lived in Clock House opposite the post office and died in 2000. He claimed to be our oldest inhabitant. He grew vegetables, selling them from the back of his van over a wide area. For the Tisbury Jubilee book, Toby produced a photograph of his father's butcher's shop where he was born in 1906. It occupied the premises which is now Boots the chemists. It shows the Christmas preparations in 1925. Four cattle, bought in Salisbury market, had been driven up the High Street to be slaughtered by Toby and Billy Jay in one of the three slaughterhouses in the village – theirs was behind the shop. The carcasses were hung up in front of the shop as a Christmas show, together with many poultry which had to be fetched down from the frontage with a long pole. Meat was also displayed outside on tables.

The shop had been built like all the others by Archibald Beckett (see page 34) and, when there was a period of only about 15 years to run, the trades people got together and bought the leases out. I can remember that my father Jack Shallcross was the valuer for the freeholders. I would remind everyone that, before the High Street was built, the road ran down the Causeway, behind what were to become the High Street shops.

Paul Robinson followed Paul Wishart and when he ceased trading, a new butcher took over. He was Bob Palmer, who started his business in Tisbury in 1996 having already started trading as Manor Farm Meats at Burcombe. Our present butcher Lee Downer came from Ferndown where he learnt his trade at a local high street butchers from the age of 16. He then pursued a retail management career at Safeway's before returning to butchery by managing Bob Palmer's shop until 2005, when he bought the business from him.

Lee employs five ladies from the village part-time. A large percentage of meat is still cut up on the premises, although you won't see cow carcasses hung in the window! Lee buys most of the meat from Owtons in the New Forest; apart from the usual joints he will sell whole lambs jointed to order and will trade in whatever people want, including goat meat. He is open seven days a week.

Lee has expanded his business to include the sale of vegetables and pet food. Pies are brought in from Bob Palmer's premises at Burcombe which is now operated by Manor Farm Butchers; Bob Palmer now concentrates on the catering business.

Quite recently Lee's wife Donna has taken the lease of Gillingham's Old Coal Shop and has established a very unusual business called Tisbury Style Exchange. This is a clothing agency where ladies can bring in clothing which is no longer needed and is sold by Donna for them on commission. Handbags and shoes are also sold. Lee and Donna's youngest daughter, Gracie, manages the shop; she is taking an apprenticeship in shop management. She has two older sisters, Asher and Stacey, and also two younger brothers, Tyler and Kai. They live in Gillingham.

So far Tisbury is not threatened by a supermarket and Lee says that the Co-op brings a lot of trade into the village. This greatly benefits his own sales. We are extremely fortunate in being served by such dedicated shopkeepers and we hope that they will continue to thrive in the future.

I understand that it was reported that the present pope Francis, when asked as a youth what he wanted to be, said 'a butcher'.

March 2016

Public Houses

The very welcome revival of the Royal Oak public house in Swallowcliffe got me thinking about the role of pubs in our community.

Because we are close to the main roads from London to the south-west, some of the local pubs serviced the needs of travellers in the days before cars. The old road from Salisbury to Shaftesbury ran through Salisbury racecourse along the crest of the downs south of Swallowcliffe, and the needs of travellers were served by a few lonely so-called 'huts'. The Fovant Hut still survives as a house.

The A30, as it was later called, was then built and 'turnpiked' from 1788 to 1864. The costs of building and maintaining the road were recovered by charging the travellers tolls, as is the case with some modern motorways.

Pubs alongside the road included the London Elm at Swallowcliffe, demolished within living memory, and the King's Elm in Compton Chamberlayne, now a private house. This pub and the two at Fovant also looked after the inner needs of the many Australians who were stationed nearby in the camps under the downs. It was said that Mrs Lovell, the licensee of the King's Elm from 1915 to 1920, used to fill a bath with beer just before the Australians came off duty so that they could scoop up their first pints in a tankard and down them very quickly as was their custom. The two pubs at Fovant closed but I am told that the Pembroke Arms is to be revived soon as a restaurant.

The pubs in the villages served a different function. When we started farming in the 1950s there were many farm labourers in each village and very few had cars. Most would slake their thirst in a nearby pub, like the Benett Arms at East Hatch, after the end of a hard day's work on the land. There were no TVs and few people wanted to drink at home.

In the 1950s I used to go round in an ancient Land Rover to all the pubs in the area trying to drum up local darts teams to enter the farmers' winter league. The idea was that the local farmer, who by that time had some form of mechanical transport, would pick up his men and take part in the match at each pub in the area. This provided for some good socialising and a bit of bonding between the bosses and the men.

Ted Woods, one of our farm workers, acquired an old Morris car. Very daringly he drove out of the village, somehow managing the hills, to have a pint at the Crown at Alvediston. In those days the village was called 'Helluva distance'.

One by one we have seen pubs close including the Cribbage Hut, later the Lancers, on the A30 at Sutton Mandeville. That was built between the wars as a roadhouse but the de-trunking of the A30 eventually finished it off, and now people stop at the Little Chef on the A303 at Willoughby Hedge.

The Royal Oak at Swallowcliffe was named after the oak in which the future King Charles II hid after the Battle of Worcester in 1651. The building has the date 1705 on one chimney and is now Grade II listed. It was originally a farmhouse and a tannery. We know that drink was being sold there in 1810 and later the tannery ceased and it became a proper alehouse in 1852.

The nearby church had been sinking into the adjoining meadow and was rebuilt on higher ground in 1840. By 1852 the Royal Oak was in full swing, no doubt aided by the great increase in church congregations in Victorian times. One hundred and ninety people were recorded as attending morning service in the 1851 census. Then the number of communicants in the village was between 30 and 40. The prosperity of the pub and the church seemed to go rather hand in hand and I can remember when Pat Ost, then Pat Evans, used to slip across to eight o'clock services before she opened the pub on a Sunday morning. We lost the Maypole at Ansty some years ago.

The Royal Oak staggered on and Liam, the last manager, drew his last pint in 2007. The building started to deteriorate. The new owners never occupied it but tried to obtain planning permission for alternative use. This was vigorously opposed by the villagers. Eventually they put their money where their mouths were when, at Christmas 2012, the freehold was bought by local businessmen Andrew Millward, Steve Radford and Jeremy Little. Dry rot and collapsing thatch were just two of the major problems which they found and extensive repairs, renovations and extensions took three years.

The provision of a new kitchen and the Oak Room dining room now mean that 60 to 70 people can be served food. The chef/patron is Mark Treasure who used to run the Museum Inn at Farnham. Phase Two will involve the conversion of the old stables into a function room and additional workspaces. The pub is a major local employer with 30 mainly part-time people on the payroll.

Being owned by villagers, the pub is very much angled to the needs of the village. The resident beer is called Cliffehanger from Butcombe Brewery and our local Keystone is sometimes a guest beer. The furniture was all designed and made by Matthew Burt of Hindon.

The Royal Oak is a very rare example of an old pub, threatened with conversion to residential use, being saved for the social benefit of the locality. As one of the owners told me, 'It just had to be done, regardless of cost.' I cannot tell you what the work did cost, but I know that it was way over budget and the owners are to be congratulated on a marvellous result!

The natural world

February 2005

Forestry

I t is nearly two years since I last wrote about trees and I return to them because they are so important in our landscape. It is in the winter that we can see the shape of their trunks and branches. As I drive along, I mentally thin and prune trees near the road. As a nation we are quite good at planting trees but then we seem to neglect them. Small trees need to be spaced no less than two metres apart so as not to compete with each other and then need to be thinned regularly from about 10 years onwards. If this is not done carefully, selecting the trees which will grow on for 100 years or so, they will damage each other in the wind. They will become spindly and useless. I admire the way the French care for the trees in the avenues along their roads so that they grow safely to a mature height. They are a great feature of their landscape. I do wish that our landowners would do the same. The French also seemed to grow lots of mistletoe in their trees.

I had a good look around our four-acre copse after Christmas. It is ancient woodland with oak planted in the southern half and ash, which has been coppiced, in the northern half. Hazel forms the understory. A hundred years ago, the timber from the copse – each farm had one – would have been greatly valued by the Wardour estate as a renewable source of firewood as well as materials for buildings, fencing, hurdles and perhaps charcoal. The best 'stems' of oak and ash were felled many years ago. Those of the oaks that remain are rougher specimens. They are perhaps 150 years old and each covers a radius of about 30 metres with its branches. They will remain as gigantic living things of great value to all sorts of wildlife. The small trees growing below them can come out for firewood but the cordwood needs to dry outside for about two years before it will burn without gumming up the chimney with tar. We've felled and kept one straight stem in the hope that it may eventually turn into a dining room table.

Many specimen trees grow largely unnoticed in our woods. More obviously in our field to the right of the Wardour Road near the railway land stands a venerable Scots pine and an oak both on the diagonal land line of a very old bank. I have been told that this was the ancient boundary of Cranborne Chase. A photograph of this Scots pine with Wick Farm behind it was printed in a beautiful book published by the Compton Press which operated from the old Brewery for a few years. Someone may have a copy. Other notable visible local trees are the fine limes near Wardour School and the Wellingtonia avenue between Pyt House and Semley. Trees take a lot of space and are expensive to remove when they overgrow gardens. It recently cost £300 to cut and remove one ornamental cypress that a gardener had planted too close to his own backdoor about 40 years ago.

Rooks still nest in the alder trees orders growing along the banks of the river Nadder near the farm. I have heard that a heap of small potatoes were found under an oak tree used as a rookery in North Wales many years ago. They were exactly the same size as rooks' eggs and were believed to have been used by the birds to make sure that their nests were of the right capacity for their eggs.

August 2006

Fishing in the Nadder

The River Nadder flows through our valley. Its headwaters are not far away in Semley and Donhead; the tiny Sem and Don meet just opposite the old shop at Wardour, a short distance beyond Wardour School.

The river at Wallmead looks rather uninviting. It is hemmed in by alder trees with a black clay bottom; the water level is well below the banks and it is waist-deep.

It comes to life briefly as it passes the farmhouse where it is fast and shallow. This stretch is called Monmouth's Ford and the little bullheads, caddis fly larvae and other minute living things are fascinating. Richard Dawkins reading from his books at the Salisbury Festival gave a riveting account of how the caddis fly larvae make their dry stone cocoons out of tiny pebbles, rotating each one to fit. 'Why do we think we are so clever?' was his message.

Two miles of the Nadder as well as the lakes at Ark Farm, Wardour and Dinton are fished by the Tisbury Angling Club which, in its present form, dates from 1964. It is one of our largest communal activities, rivalling the churches and sports clubs. There are 156 senior members and 34 juniors under 16. The annual subscriptions are very modest so everyone can afford to join. Juniors only pay £5 per annum, so couch potatoes and internet boffins get out and enjoy some fresh air by the water. It is not just about catching fish and putting them back again. A whole new world inhabits river banks; you might even see an otter or a kingfisher! All inland fishermen must also have a licence from the Environment Agency, which can be bought at the Tisbury post office.

There are wild brown trout and grayling in the Nadder which may be eaten if caught with a fly. The bony coarse fish are mainly roach, chub, barbel, bream and dace, caught with worms for bait. The tiny gudgeons present a particular challenge. The record for them, established in 1969 by D. Jack and equalled in 1985 by G. Bull, is an impressive '3oz 11drams'. They would only be a starter if they somehow strayed into Dinton Lake and met the record 22lb pike. Even larger was a 25lb carp also from Dinton. Eels are now quite scarce but the record is 6lb taken from Wardour Lake. Incidentally some names come up regularly in the record book, especially Mark Howell. I should also pay tribute to two of the many people who have guided the management of the club over the years: Eddie Stevens of Fovant is the veteran of them all and more recently Paddy Douglas-Pennant has been the chairman.

Because of the policies of the club it is very much a community resource. By contrast much of the lower Nadder nearer to Salisbury is fished by illustrious fly fishing syndicates with mown banks, keepers, large annual subs and a waiting list.

The Nadder, while providing little food for humans, supports an important ecosystem and has provided several local students with material for exam studies. Water volume and quality are vital. The fish take cover for their lives when the river floods over its banks several times a year. The fragile tributaries from Fonthill and Teffont are monitored constantly to ensure that the water extraction from the bore-holes just north of Fonthill Bishop do not denude the aquifers in the chalk. Water is perhaps the most precious of all the natural resources.

December 2006

Quarries of Dorset and south Wiltshire

T he great slice of stone cake that is the Isle of Portland is joined to the rest of the Dorset Jurassic coast by the mysterious Chesil (old English: shingle) Beach which is attached to the mainland at Abbotsbury swannery eight miles to the west.

The geological name for a bank like this is a tombolo. The seams of Portland stone plunge deep below the Dorset chalk downs to reappear unexpectedly, with the adjacent Purbeck stone, 40 miles to the north in the Nadder Valley. Could we call it the Jurassic Valley?

There are about fifty fossil zones in the Jurassic of varying thicknesses, each laid down over about 600,000 years; some under the sea, containing fossils such as ammonites and Tisbury coral and some when the land was above water revealing fossilised wood and dinosaurs. Quarries are complicated places, although a clever geologist might be able to decode the rock sequences in the stone walls of our houses.

The reason why the Portland and Purbeck stone is exposed all around us is because of an enormous eruption of the earth along the line of the Nadder millions of years ago, called an anticline. It reaches from Barford St Martin to Semley. This formed a ridge with the strata sloping upward on each side. The brittleness of the ridge allowed it to be eroded into a V and eventually the Nadder was formed to drain the hills on either side eastwards. The strata on either side of the valley match each other.

When Salisbury Cathedral was built in the 13th century it was more convenient to quarry the stone locally than to bring it from France or elsewhere. Although it is often said that the stone came from Chilmark, there is strong speculation that it was taken from quarries along Tisbury Row especially from the area called Dumplings Down. Could the thousands of tons of stone have been floated down the Nadder? The roads must have been atrocious.

In 1846 there were forty stone quarries in the valley. Jack Green who lived and worked at Tuckingmill until the 1970s was, for a time, the last of the local quarrymen. Others now quarry and prepare stone in the valley for building and ornamental purposes. The closest of these operations to Tisbury is the open-faced quarry in Upper Chicksgrove at Pophams (now Quarry) Farm. This was already in operation in 1412 when it was called Barry's. Busy in the 19th century, it was then abandoned for many years and bought by RMC to extract waste material for road building. When Ron Collins retired in 1986 he bought the quarry and started to extract fine building stone again. Today it is the principal source for Salisbury Cathedral's ongoing repair programme. Ron died in 1999 and his wife Sally has been in charge ever since. One of their sons, William, obtained a degree in Mining and Quarrying from the Camborne School of Mines and is employed in the quarry with manager Bill Maynard and three other men.

The building stone is only about two metres thick and lies under 13 metres of overburden stone which is of practically no value. It is called Tisbury Member and is divided into four beds. The stone blocks are either sawn on three sides for special building projects or guillotined for ordinary use. Stone has recently been supplied for rebuilding Ferne Park and extending Fonthill House.

The demand for local stone is now high and is increasingly specified for new houses in south Wilts where good stonemasons are to be found. A few years ago reconstructed stone was favoured for cheapness but it is much inferior in appearance, as can be seen at Wallmead where we also have one of Jack Green's splendid mullions.

The Collins family have left Tisbury. The Chicksgrove quarry has been greatly expanded and is operated by Lovell Purbeck Ltd. I have enjoyed taking groups of interested people to inspect it, strictly by appointment.

January 2008

Wiltshire Wildlife and the Woodland Trust

Habitat is the name of a rather up-market shop but it really means the natural environment within which a single species lives. Often we use it to describe the physical conditions within which many species live, but technically this should be called a biotope. I will stay with biotope so we can be a bit snobbish and might even score an extra point in the pub quiz.

I lift the corner of the old carpet which covers the biotope which is my triple compost heap. It steams with heat and is heaving with all sorts of invertebrates and sometimes a mouse or a slow-worm. By the time it is ready for spreading they have all moved on, leaving the fruits of their digestive systems to pep up my topsoil. Our own digestive systems are also a very well-populated biotope, teeming with bacteria.

I say this to point out that most of the species of wildlife are virtually invisible to the casual observer but fascinating to the specialist. Our woodland is, or can be, particularly rich in species and we naturally concentrate on the very visible ones.

Several local woods belong to conservation charities such as the RSPB, the Woodland Trust (which owns Ambrose Copse, Semley) and the Wiltshire Wildlife Trust which bought the nearby 22-acre Oysters Coppice at Gutch Common 12 years ago with funds raised from a campaign led by Bishop John Bickersteth. The Trust had managed it for 15 years before then. About a dozen volunteers join the wardens on the first Sunday of each month coppicing hazel, thinning ash, holly, oak and birch trees, improving the drainage, laying hedges, maintaining the paths and pond and many other tasks. Rarities among the bird population are the marsh tit, lesser spotted woodpecker and nuthatch.

This wood has a particular link with Tisbury because Andrew and Debbie Carter have been the wardens for the last seven years. The reserve is open to the public all the year round with a carefully maintained circular walk. I visited in December with the leaves carpeting the ground on a stormy day when the chairman of the managing committee had been surprised to see a large cat of puma-like appearance crossing a path which he walks along daily with his dog.

Boxes on trees encourage nesting birds and dormice. The wood is carpeted with bluebells and wild daffodils in the spring; later there are banks of very smelly wild garlic – good for salads, I was told. Specialist advice from the Trust is always at hand as the trees are subject to a Tree Preservation Order. The wood is part of a SSSI (Site of Special Scientific interest).

The lower part of the steep site has a yellow clay subsoil causing many springs to gush out from the greensand which overlies it; this makes the management a very difficult task as virtually all work has to be done by hand. Pushing a wheelbarrow laden with tools to the gate by the road at the top of the site after a heavy storm was a testing task. More willing slaves would be welcomed. Our primary school is one of six that visit the wood and find a myriad of things to explore even when the badgers and deer have taken cover and the owls are in bed.

Oysters Coppice is a beautiful home with layers of biotopes allowing an enormous diversity of species to flourish. Do make a resolution to visit in the spring.

Finally New Year's blessings, hoping that the biotope of your digestive system coped well with the festive excesses.

February 2009

The Arundells – Quarrying in Cornwall

A curving section of the stone wall at the entrance to Quarry Farm, Chicksgrove collapsed years ago and the heap of rubble was covered with nettles but I unearthed sound foundations. John Needham has just rebuilt the wall using lime mortar having found most of the original curved stones. They were cut and shaped from Portland deposits in the adjoining quarry in 1840 when the listed farm buildings were erected. I took photos before and after and John was so pleased with the result that he kept on thanking me for asking him to do the work.

Our local geology is relatively straightforward as far as the 70-million-year-old upper chalk downs to north and south are concerned, but the Vale of Wardour has a fascinating history. Don't miss John Needham's presentation to the Wiltshire Wildlife Trust on the 145-million-year-old Jurassic Period at 7.30pm on 12 March at the Hinton Hall.

To find more complicated geology you drive south-west as far from Tisbury as you can go: 175 miles to the Penwith peninsula. The rebuilt A30 dual carriageway beyond Exeter gets you there in less than four hours but in geological time you go rather slowly, well over one million years per mile. All the later rocks have been eroded there so what you see is very old and very complicated indeed. Tin and copper were mined there for centuries.

St Michael's Mount is a rock that has resisted the sea and we walked the shining stone causeway just as it was exposed by the morning tide. The Normans came and gave it to the monks of Mont Saint-Michel who owned it until the reign of Henry V. It is on a much smaller scale than its very commercialised French cousin and is quietly managed by the National Trust.

Our local Arundell family of Wardour is Cornish and at one time owned a considerable part of that county. Sir John Arundell of Trerice died on the sands attacking the Mount during the Wars of the Roses. A later Arundell, Humphrey, rebelled against the use of new 1547 prayer book in English and also laid successful siege to the Mount. However, the rebellion was snuffed out near Exeter and he was captured and hanged at Tyburn. Also in 1547 Sir Thomas Arundell of Lanherne bought the Wardour estate and wisely did not enter the West Country rebellion. Sadly he was wrongly accused of taking part in a plot and he too was executed in 1552. Dangerous times.

In the 1850s the London and South-Western Railway Company reached Tisbury and stretched its tentacles down to the Atlantic coast terminating its tracks at places like Padstow and Ilfracombe. It reached the slate quarry at Delabole which belonged to the then Lord Arundell who sent a truck of the greenish slates to Tisbury to re-roof Wallmead which was previously thatched. We saw similar slates on the roof of the 19th-century Truro Cathedral where the stone flooring is a study in itself. The Victorian builders also remodelled the east elevation of Wallmead, built on a smart little porch and floored it with a 5 feet by 3 feet slab of local Oolitic Purbeck stone. Oolites mean eggs and the stone is made up of thousands of fossils which look like eggs. They framed the stone with decorative tiles which also surround our fireplace.

Delabole quarry has just supplied 50 newly quarried Cornish slates so we can repair our roof (March 2017).

July 2009

John Needham – the Jurassic period

Wiltshire Wildlife followed up John Needham's lecture on the Jurassic Period in the Nadder Valley with a field visit to the quarry to see where he had discovered a large fossilised tree, now at the Natural History Museum.

John Needham took us to a plateau overlooking the quarry where about a metre of modern topsoil had been removed to uncover the dark soil of the Purbeck beds where the 145-million-year-old tree had been found. We walked between white domes, about the size of those old coppers that granny used boil clothes in on Mondays. Those in the know murmured 'stromatolites'. I was completely ignorant so took some photos and googled. I found that for two billion years primitive algae and bacteria were the only life forms on earth. They grew under the sea and formed mattresses with carbonates, some of which later fossilised into hard nodules, the oldest fossils found. The ones we saw were roughly the same age as John's tree but some still grow today in super saline bays off the coast of Western Australia and in a few other places.

The point is that these algae spent three billion years converting the original carbon dioxide atmosphere of the earth into oxygen and this enabled life, which needs oxygen, to evolve. I wanted to go back, fall on my knees and cry 'Mother' but something stopped me.

June 2010

Managing the countryside

If you are a member of Wiltshire Wildlife Trust, one of the publications you will receive is *Natural World,* the magazine of the Wildlife Trusts of England.

The spring edition contains a lovely picture of a water vole close to a public footpath in County Durham. Two weeks ago we were in Salisbury on a Saturday afternoon. The footpath next to the town mill was full of people looking at ducks and their ducklings sitting on a raft of water weed which had collected by the hatches. A few of us saw, in the corner next to Polly's Tea Rooms, a large water vole below us snuffling around happily and taking no notice of any one.

When we came to Wallmead over 60 years ago, the banks of the Nadder was lined with their holes and a walk along the river produced lots of plopping sounds as they heard us coming and dived in. It is said that their almost total extinction in the Nadder has been due to mink that escaped from mink farms.

The countryside needs to be managed. To do this needs a lot of research, an agreed plan and a deep pocket. There are many examples of this. Deer numbers would increase to an impossible extent if they were not culled regularly. Much research is being done now to control badger numbers so that they do not get infected with TB and in turn infect the many dairy cows which are currently being killed each week in the West Country. Foxes have to be shot to protect new-born lambs.

We farmers are paid big subsidies to leave the margins of fields uncultivated as a habitat for ground-nesting birds. This means that we cannot drive vehicles over the margins. People and especially dogs have to be discouraged from walking on them. However, the major problem is predators, like crows, which wait for the ground-nesting birds to lay their eggs and then pillage them. Crows can only be controlled by professionals like gamekeepers; there are few such around nowadays and they are mainly confined to the big shooting estates. In the past there was a rather sad string in each wood upon which the conscientious keeper would hang the withered bodies of magpies, crows, jays and predatory animals such as stoats.

We naturally favour some species over others: witness the control of grey squirrels and American crayfish to preserve our threatened native breeds. Wolves and beavers are being reintroduced, otters are back here and flourishing and the red kite can be seen in our valley.

The Game Conservancy Trust, based at Fordingbridge, is the leading research body looking into these matters. In order to encourage the water voles to return, experiments being conducted use floating platforms (clay stuck on Oasis) to detect mink footprints. Where the mink are found to be present, special traps can be used in order to catch and destroy them.

Years ago, the whole of south-west Wilts was in a rabbit clearance area. Trappers were employed to control the hordes of bunnies which destroyed acres of crops on each farm. I always suspected that the trappers left a few pairs of rabbits here and there to breed and so keep themselves in business. In the late 1950s, myxomatosis virtually finished off the rabbits.

Perhaps in a few years' time gamekeepers will be employed at a parish level to control predators that, more than agricultural cultivations, are destroying the breeding prospects of birds. None of us local farmers could afford to employ a gamekeeper on our own. Where they exist, they are working for syndicate shoots which cover several farms, but these have been affected by the credit crunch.

On a completely separate note Jenny is reading a book about the family of Edward Thomas, the poet. Members of his family came on foot to visit Arthur Ransome who was living in a farmhouse at Hatch. His wife was called Ivy and their daughter Tabitha but Ransome was in Russia at the time skating on the frozen Volga with Lenin's daughter. MI6 recruited him as a spy. He married Trotsky's secretary and his spying made him rich enough to buy a yacht. They moved to the Lake District and *Swallows and Amazons* was written in 1930. I expect that the Hatch connection is recorded in the local history archives.

I doubt if dragons ever stalked this land but I now have one as a computer programme. It has typed most of this article as I have dictated it through a microphone. It has taught me to speak v e r y d i s t i n c t l y to it. It makes few mistakes and spells better than me. It tries hard to make sense of steel, stele or steal. It cost £45 and is called Dragon Naturally Speaking 10. It is friendly with Amazon, where it can be bought.

November 2012

Our stony pastures – Higher Level Stewardship Scheme

I have whinged in these articles over many years about the poor quality of our arable land. In one particular field at Teffont near the railway line it is virtually impossible to walk without turning your ankle as the stones are almost touching.

In other places the depth of soil over solid stone is only about nine inches. The nature of the soil itself also means that the yield of cereals is always depressed, and in a difficult season like the current one, it has again been demonstrated that it is hardly worth sowing wheat on some fields.

Happily there is a solution because the generous acreage grants from the European Union are being reduced annually by modulation and given back to those who seriously want to preserve wildlife and habitats in our countryside.

Our son Peter has always been keen on wildlife, and butterflies in particular, and he has taken advantage of the so-called Higher Level Stewardship Scheme of the EU to sign up over 10 years to an extensive programme of habitat improvement on the thousand acres we farm.

I apologise for giving you a lot of statistics about it, but the scale of the work involved emphasises how extensive the scheme has to be to qualify for the grants which will now run at about £30,000 per annum and will provide a useful part of the farm income as well as hopefully improving the local environment.

- Selective hedge management means that normally hedges are only trimmed back about every three years apart from along roads.

- Fifty acres of cereal fields are left uncultivated in stubble until February to encourage wildlife. After we have eventually harvested our 85 acres of forage maize in October, the land will be cultivated to avoid rapid run-off of heavy rain from the compacted land.

- We have planted a further 15 acres of wild bird seed mixture and are leaving this unharvested for the seed-eating finches.

- Another 10 acres will be left for ground-nesting birds, especially lapwings; margins are carefully cultivated (but not cropped) to encourage plant species which would normally be called weeds.

- Six-metre wide strips round all the arable fields, a very large area, will be taken out of production so that rough grass and flowers can be encouraged and, in some of the arable fields, corners will be left, amounting to about 10 acres, to encourage tufty grass.

- Nectar mixes will be a sown in the shape of legumes in about 10 acres for bumblebees, and permanent grassland will be farmed in such a way as to increase the number of species over a wide area. Other areas will be farmed so as to encourage flowers.

Grants have been provided for 5km of sheep fencing and new hedges planted to encourage the foraging bats that live in caves in the former RAF Chilmark.

Chantry Field is about 45 acres overlooking Tisbury. It is fortunate that there is no footpath across it so management in the ways I have described can be conducted without interference by humans. Even so the large area in the middle of the field has to be fenced off to keep out foxes and any straying dogs, and allow lapwings to nest undisturbed. There were seven nests this year.

The management of our land for conservation is of interest to other farmers and at a recent farm Open Day it was gratifying that when we cautiously drove on a tractor and trailer into the corner of Chantry Field, a group of lapwings were wheeling around at the far end.

As I said, this is a ten-year scheme and we are only in year two. It will be fascinating to see whether the large sums of money we receive over the whole period and the very specialist work we carry out will result in real improvements to the environment.

The food chain is extremely complicated and starts with the tiniest forms of life invisible to the eye and only ends up with the species that we can actually see ourselves. So the results are not always obvious.

Returning to the present, the rain came down with a vengeance at the beginning of October and the cows have had to be housed permanently about a month early. At the time of writing the maize crop is still standing in waterlogged ground. We can only hope that this vital winter food can be successfully clamped and will last until April when the cows can go back onto grass again.

April 2014

Death of a veteran Scots pine

We have lost the veteran Scots pine that stood alone in the meadow, clearly visible from the road from Wardour and from the nearby railway. The foliage had been dying back year by year and the trunk was hollow. It used to be a nesting site of a Little Owl but we have not seen it for many years.

I knew that the pine's days were numbered but was not prepared for the mighty storm on the Friday night in February that toppled it. I measured it as it lay on the ground. It was 65 feet high and the diameter measured 10 feet near its base. It has now been cut up and several people have attempted to count the rings. They are extremely close together near the outside as it had put on very little girth over the last fifty years. We reckon that it was probably at least 230 years old, which means that it was planted in the late 1700s. It was one of several trees which grew along the bank which I'm told was the original boundary of Cranborne Chase. One of the glossy publications of W.H. Hudson's *A Shepherd's Life* includes a photograph of Tisbury church with our Scots pine in the foreground. It is therefore preserved for posterity in print.

Another casualty was the young oak tree which I had planted at the end of our garden thirty years ago. It had grown to about 25 feet in height. I had cared for this tree and was very fond of it because it framed the view from the house up to the high ground beyond. On St Jude's day last October the sudden storm shattered this tree, although the trunk was quite sound. The wood is all now logged and stacked up German-style in my woodshed ready to be burnt in a year's time, but the tree would never have made useable timber as it had a twisted form.

Most of us who use the A30 will have been concerned about the state of the high conifers on the right-hand side of the road near the Heath Farm mobile home site near Barford St Martin. I can remember when these cupressus trees were planted perhaps fifty years ago as nurse trees to a row of beech which were designed to form half of an avenue. Unfortunately, having planted the two species of tree, the owners seemed to have neglected them. The conifers should have been thinned and then removed many years ago and the beech pruned and encouraged to form straight mature trees.

During last winter the now enormous conifers blew across the road one by one, taking the telegraph wires with them each time. Perhaps 15 trees came down and I think that they hit at least one car. The road was frequently closed to clear the debris. Eventually in March all the remaining conifers were taken out across the adjoining field; this would have cost thousands of pounds. The remaining beech trees are mainly poor forked specimens. The moral is that trees near roads need careful management.

In England we are not very good at looking after trees. We are enthusiastic planters but much less diligent in thinning and pruning trees to the best advantage. Tree cover in this country is less than in most parts of Europe. I am a member of the Royal Forestry Society and we have a variety of interesting summer meetings out in the woods. Some woodland, such as that at Stourhead, is beautifully managed, but many of our wooded areas are neglected. We owners have a reasonable excuse: thinning and pruning is extremely expensive and the market value of standing timber is uncertain, though the value of firewood is strengthening as wood-burners become more popular.

In the end it all comes down to a matter of pride and landowners caring for woods which should be the glory of our countryside. Perhaps it is better not to have too critical of view of these things and just to enjoy nature in its apparently natural state. I say 'apparently' because there are few areas of entirely natural woodland; nearly all of it was planned and planted by our forebears.

December 2014

Fossil trees and the Harwell Synchrotron

J ohn Needham, Tisbury stonemason and geologist, published his book *Forests of the Dinosaurs, Wiltshire's Jurassic Finale* in 2011 (Hobnob Press and available in Tisbury post office). It was based on his research of the layers of stone in the Chicksgrove quarry just east of Tisbury. Some of the strata contained the remains of trees and the dinosaurs which lived about 145 million years ago. The dinosaurs were extinguished approximately 80 million years later and pre-existed the trees by many million years. By comparison man, a recent arrival, has only walked the planet for a tiny fraction of the era of the dinosaurs.

John excavated a large fossilised tree which was taken to the Natural History Museum in 2009. The last illustration in his book, before the postscript, is a picture of one of two small fossilised tree cones which he found in crevices in the limestone rocks in the quarry. At the time he was unable to identify the cones and therefore the tree specimen, so his book ended with a question.

Now there is an amazing new scientific tool called the Diamond Light Source; it is a 'synchrotron' half a kilometre in diameter situated at Harwell near Didcot in Oxfordshire. If you are of a scientific mind you may like to look up the research on the web. The synchrotron looks like a football stadium, and the public can visit it.

This amazing X-ray machine, in which electrons circulate at near the speed of light, was able to study the cones and in particular the ovules (seeds) trapped in them. We have lots of similar fossilised wood around the farm and my mother always told me that they were a species of monkey puzzle, *auraucaria*, which naturally occurs these days in South America but can be bought in garden centres and is found in local gardens. Forty-one species are known to grow today.

Indeed the specimen was identified accurately and is a new species, *para-auraucaria collinsonae*. This is the first identified specimen of the extinct conifer genus *para-auraucaria* in Europe. At the time of the Jurassic era, when this one was growing, the only other examples recorded so far were in Argentina and the western USA. At the time south Wiltshire had a dry, arid Mediterranean-type climate and was a low-lying coastal area.

Also at the time, Argentina was on the Gondwana plate and we were on the Laurasia. There was an ocean between us. For the species to be growing in these locations so far apart we must surmise that they came from a common source, many million years before, when the earth mass formed a single continent.

The Diamond Light Source will no doubt be of great value in telling us far more about the long history of this planet which hitherto has only been determined from the examination of the fossil records. My mother must have had recourse to some earlier expertise!

November 2015

Roman remains

When we first started farming in Tisbury in 1949, tractors had just taken over from horses, although we kept two carthorses for winter work. The tractors' narrow tyres made terrible ruts in the land when it was wet. In 1953 the tractors were Fordson Majors which were fairly sophisticated at that time yet still had no hydraulics. Our champion ploughman Ted Rixon was ploughing Chantry Field overlooking the station in the week of the Queen's coronation in 1953. Because of the thin soil in this field, he was therefore proceeding rather gingerly when the plough hit something and jolted the tractor to a stop. It had moved a large slab of rock which had broken into two. Going back to investigate, Ted found a cavity in which he could see bones.

The police were called but pronounced the bones to be at least 1,500 years old and therefore of no interest to them. The hole was excavated and a coffin carved out of one piece of local stone was revealed with the remains of a body together with dog bones and nails found to be from Roman sandals. The bones were removed and in their place lay Steve Rogers in his school uniform. A photograph of him was taken and is included in Rex Sawyer's *The Tisbook 1900–2005*. The coffin itself can be viewed at Shaftesbury Museum.

It is not surprising that the grave was so shallow because just below it are many metres of solid rock. It required a battery of modern hydraulic diggers to slice through it a few years ago when the Donhead sewer pumping main was laid through the field on its way to our sewage works.

Nowadays we are not allowed to bury any animals at all on the farm and any casualties have to be taken away at considerable cost and disposed of. However, those who till the soil can still be buried on their land provided the remains are not close to a watercourse.

The churchyard at St John's Tisbury has been full for many years and closed for burials. Only ashes can be buried there now and space is at a premium. When I am to conduct a little service for the burial of ashes, I like to dig the small holes for the reception of the ashes myself. It is quite a good way of meditating about life and death. My parents' ashes are close by. There may be 30,000 human bodies buried in our churchyard, considering it has been used for 800 years. It is only comparatively recently that people have afforded stones and so the old remains are unrecorded. Last month I dug out a lower jawbone, with much better teeth than mine, only about 18 inches from the surface.

We are told that the cost of funerals has increased by 80 per cent over the last 10 years. In a recent interview on Sunday morning with funeral directors' representatives they failed to point out that we can all buy a funeral plan well in advance to save our relatives having to fork out possibly £5,000. Having taken out a funeral plan, however, you are tied to the business who sold it to you. They may at that time have been a local family-owned and run business, but by the time the plan matures on your death they could be part of a large chain. The necessary extras could prove to be expensive. Recently a lady was widowed with no money by an unreliable husband. She told me that the cheapest funeral she could possibly arrange through a family-run firm had cost her £2,800.

On the other hand a consultant at our hospital died a few years ago and his family decided to make all the arrangements themselves. I was asked to call at the house one Sunday when I found him lying in state in his open coffin, bought on the internet, in his dining room. The family, including his grandchildren, had gathered to say goodbye and were putting notes in with him. He was a Quaker so I said a few words and we had a good silence. When they arrived at Salisbury Crematorium the family brought the coffin, which had been in the hospital mortuary, in one of their cars and carried him into the chapel. A short suitable service was devised by them. They found the authorities such as the registrar of deaths and the staff at the crematorium were so helpful that the assistance of a funeral director was not needed.

I must say I found the whole thing very refreshing and natural, and reflected on the fact that until about 150 years ago this would have been the normal way of dealing with things, with the help of the local carpenter, rather than the internet, for the supply of the coffin.

That Roman coffin must have cost a fortune to have chiselled out. It is a real work of art. Excavating the grave and burying the very heavy coffin must have involved a large team of strong people. We will never know who the occupant of it was and what his relationship to our farm might have been. When my time comes I know of another field where the digging will be easy!

October 2016

A few scientific notes

I was interested to read recently that geologists in Greenland had uncovered a very old bed of stromatolites. These are one of the earliest forms of life: algae that convert carbon dioxide in the atmosphere into oxygen. They have suggested that the bed is about two billion years older than the previous estimates of 1.3 billion years.

I have a small stromatolite sitting on my drive. It is a local Jurassic example only about 145 million years old. Recently a large bed of its cousins was uncovered at Chicksgrove quarry. All of this is very recent compared to the origin of our universe which started with a Big Bang about 14 billion years ago.

We also recently read that the earth and moon once formed a single mass which was vaporised by a massive collision with a planet-sized object, causing the moon to be separated from the earth before both became solid again.

One reminder of the age of our universe is the snowstorm effect on our screens when we switch our televisions on. This permanent white snowstorm is caused by cosmic microwave radiation released by the Big Bang. It will presumably continue until the Big Bang is somehow reversed and matter ends. It was identified by American scientists in 1964; they were awarded the Nobel Prize for their explanation in 1978.

It all reminds us how short our lifespan is and how powerless we are to have any effect on the universe itself. As far as our planet is concerned, we know that man can cause potentially fatal (for human beings) changes to the atmosphere, the long-term effect of which we cannot yet determine.

I will be shortly taking another group around the farm and the quarry to look at the great upheaval which took place about 65 million years ago when the African tectonic plate collided violently with the Eurasian plate to push up the Alps. Only recently the same effect on a much smaller scale was suffered in the Umbrian region of Italy.

When the ripple effect of the Alpine 'orogeny', the movements of the earth's plates, took place, it even affected our valley. The layers of chalk of the Cretaceous era, which ended about 65 million years ago and covered much of Wiltshire and Dorset, were shattered along the length of the Vale of Wardour by the compression of the layers underneath which were forced up through the chalk. This brought up above the surface the Purbeck and Portland beds below. These had been laid down in the Jurassic era, which lasted for about 54 million years and ended around 146 million years ago. This so-called 'anticline' resulted in the same formations being pushed up on either side of our valley. The tree-covered greensand ridges at Donhead and Wardour to our south, and Fonthill and Ridge to the north mirror each other, as do the stone outcrops between them which have given us our local building materials.

This means that on our sloping land at Wallmead we can find four soil types over a distance of about 400 metres on the surface. This affects the timing of cultivations and the likely success of cropping different species on the land. None of the soil types on our land is particularly fertile and so wheat is seldom an option. Naturally the land grows plentiful grass and this year we have been conserving grass throughout the summer. We have stored mountains of black silage bales in strategic places which will be eaten by the cattle during the winter. All these have had to be paid for and Sidfords, our contractors, have been busy for months at great expense. If the grass is not cut it will damage future growth in the field.

Harvest is now over and the results have been fairly good. There has indeed been a little spike in the price of corn and the weakness of the pound will help us to export more than usual. The UK is a net exporter of cereals but a large importer of proteins to balance livestock rations.

Much of this imported protein is now grown in countries such as the US where genetic modification is standard. Some of the manufacturers require non-genetically modified food and it is increasingly difficult to obtain this.

We are now preparing for autumn and winter. The cows will be out for another month or so before the 'golden hooves' of the sheep graze the pastures down into good condition for the spring growth next year.

Mostly personal

I receive some money

Many people now own metal detectors and occasionally we are asked for access to our land. We normally only allow one person to work at a time. All finds have to be given to us and belong to the landowner unless silver or gold is found, when different rules apply. Normally we let the finder keep items they have unearthed.

Last month we were handed a small collection of coins and a bronze axe head. The axe looked like a modern reproduction as it was in mint condition. However, Salisbury Museum confirmed that it was cast in the late Bronze Age so it is about 3,000 years old. The museum has many similar items and so was not interested in keeping it. Our landlord at Teffont will keep it for his private collection and reward the finder. I wonder if anyone will discover anything we made for modern farm use in 3,000 years' time that is so beautiful and functional. I doubt it!

One thing we have just built, which is useful but not beautiful, is a length of farm track from the Wardour Road to the top of the hill. This gives a good connection to Haygrove Cottage, avoiding the old sunken track that is the bridle road from Wardour to Tisbury and goes through our farmyard with its gates, muck and cows. Often the slow procession of cows wandering up the track after milking coincided with the grandchildren's school run but not any more now it has been bypassed.

My mother has celebrated her 90th birthday: 20 years in South Africa on a farm, 16 years at Alderbury and 54 years in Tisbury. As part of the celebrations she opened the new track by cutting a length of baler twine which we passed through the car windows to save her getting out!

The grass is growing well and will soon be cut for silage. We have finished sowing our spring crops including the usual big field for maize silage and, for the first time, lupins which will be harvested to provide protein for cattle feed. They are growing at Teffont and should be very colourful.

October 2007

Working as a surveyor

I have been looking back over my fifty years in the land agency profession. It sounds boring that all this time I have worked for one partnership following in my father's footsteps, but I have never had a dull moment.

My actual experience of using a theodolite and level has been limited. One rather worrying job we had was to take levels round the base of the newly built Fawley power station chimney, about the height of Salisbury Cathedral, every few months. Presumably this was so that someone could shout 'TIMBER' in time for the workers to escape should it threaten to subside into Southampton Water. It is still standing.

Spending two hours examining the structure of houses and then writing a report for a purchaser required the protection of an expensive professional liability insurance policy. After all, the purchaser had years to discover what I had missed. I was not infallible but rather easily distracted by over-friendly dogs, over-cute children and over-attentive vendors. What a joy it was to survey an empty house with no fitted carpets.

Sometimes I had a work-experience student to set up ladders, prod with my damp-meter and lift drain covers. Once a furious vendor from Farley phoned when I was back in the office to say that I was fortunate that he had not summoned me to bath his Labrador which had fallen into the septic tank; my assistant had left the cover open. One assistant came charging white-faced round the corner of a house presumably pursued by a very dangerous animal. It turned out to be a small duck.

It has been challenging to keep up with the fluctuations in values of property. Our first detached house in the New Forest with half an acre of land cost under £4,000. Forty-five years later it is probably worth, with extensions, £550,000.

Mostly, I advise owners about the management and sale of agricultural estates and the letting of houses and land. It is important to establish the right balance of friendliness and professional correctness if the agent is to do the best for the client. The old motto of the firm, 'the client is always right', was often said with gritted teeth and very occasionally I have modified my client's instructions to be fair to a tenant or employee.

Valuing agricultural tenants in and out of tenancies could be high-tension affairs. In the old days, opposing West Country valuers would take off their jackets and threaten to knock each other's block off over the value of a rick of hay. This was theatre to impress the clients. Agricultural valuers are usually good friends and we often meet at social events.

I remember a valuation in the Piddle Valley when we were told that the outgoing tenant's wife had cooked a roast lunch for us all. The snag was that we couldn't eat it until we had agreed the valuation. Miraculously it still tasted good at 7pm. Valuing machinery was relatively straightforward and dairy cows could be put through the milking parlour to be examined individually. Sheep on the Dorset downs were tricky. They were usually wild and sometimes all you saw was a line of white tails disappearing into the mist.

Valuers use ten-letter codes so that figures can be shouted to the assistant keeping the book without the client understanding and 'putting his oar in'. Sometimes it became evident that both valuers were using the same code: say CUMBERLAND where C equals 1 and D equals 0. The outgoer's valuer would take a cursory look at a lame cow and say 'RUE' to his assistant. The ingoer's would look totally shocked, take him on one side pointing out the dodgy foot, and say 'not a penny more than BND'.

Hours were spent at Michaelmas arguing over the tonnage and value of clamps of grass silage. I wrote a paper on this art which earned me a place on the national silage committee of the Agricultural Valuers' Association (motto: 'do what is right, come what may') and several appointments as an arbitrator. Once, my assistant fell into a hole of rotted silage and had to eat his pub lunch in his underpants wrapped up in my car blanket. It is no wonder that not many people have chosen this rather specialist and not very remunerative profession, but I have no regrets.

April 2012

Mother is 100

Our mother will be celebrating her hundredth birthday on 29 April. Several of you still remember her so we thought we should write this article to celebrate her first hundred years.

Daisy was born Margaret Laura Tylden on 29 April 1912 into a remote rural community in the Orange Free State in South Africa. It was only a few years after the end of the Boer War and the British government was encouraging prospective farmers from Great Britain to colonise poor areas of farmland to counterbalance the defeated Boer farmers.

Her father Geoffrey had been given a particularly difficult area of barren land. He was a bit of an adventurer who later wrote books about horses, military history and the Basuto nation whose border was only a few miles from their farm near Ladybrand. He had made a good career choice by marrying a general's daughter who had money. Cicely Abdy, my grandmother, was also a distant cousin. The family lived under very primitive conditions.

The Tyldens had four daughters of whom Daisy was the eldest. Their fourth child was a son who died, aged three. Daisy was educated by governesses and at South African boarding schools. She went to England to study medicine when she was 18. All transport those days was by Union Castle liners which sailed from Durban and Cape Town to Southampton.

Daisy soon decided that a career in medicine was not for her, though later she became a medical secretary, part-time. When her three younger sisters joined my mother in England, they settled in Salisbury where Daisy met her future husband Jack Shallcross on the tennis court. He offered her a secretarial job in his office in Salisbury and they were married in 1934 in St Martin's Church, Salisbury.

Jack's mother, a forbidding Victorian vicar's widow, owned a large redbrick house called Hillside with eight acres of land at Alderbury and she moved out to allow Jack and Daisy to live there. All the Hillside servants left at the outbreak of war apart from Maggie Costello, the faithful Irish cook, who stayed with the family for several decades. Daisy housed several unruly boy evacuees from Portsmouth and then girls from Chessington. Throughout the war, Jack was away in Somerset acquiring land for airfields.

After the war, Jack resumed his work as an auctioneer and valuer and was a partner in the firm of Rawlence and Squarey at Salisbury until he retired. When several farms on the Wardour estate came up for sale he was able to realise his long-standing ambition to own a farm. In 1949 the family moved to the 250-acre Wallmead Farm at Tisbury, for which Jack paid £70 an acre. Daisy was very involved in planning the reorganisation of the internal accommodation in the old farmhouse.

Her next sister Barbara often came to stay and eventually ended her days in Nadder Close. Daisy was a Conservative, Barbara a Liberal and the two younger sisters Betty and Kitty were Communists. Politics were never mentioned between them!

Daisy was very active in the village, becoming chairperson of the parish council. She was organiser of the Happy Circle and a member of the Flower Group. She learnt to upholster chairs and ran a successful class for many years.

Jack was not a great traveller and apart from their honeymoon in Hungary and visits to the Isle of Wight, he never left these shores again. Daisy intrepidly took the children to Brittany on holiday soon after the end of the war but most of the family holidays were spent in Cornwall.

Maggie eventually retired and Daisy and Jack were mainly alone in the farmhouse with the farm being run by a series of managers, the last being Philip Skinner, until they handed over the farm to Martin and Jenny in 1981. Jack died soon afterwards at their bungalow in Tisbury where Daisy continued to live until she was 90. Her legs then failed her and the only practical way of caring for her was for her to live in a residential nursing home. Hays House has been her home for over ten years and she is happy there.

In her late nineties her recent memory has faded but she remembers more and more of her childhood in Africa. Some of her stories are quite lurid and we have no way of assessing their veracity. She will still entertain the staff with naughty limericks!

She will preside over an open afternoon at Hays on her birthday and hopes to be visited by her five grandchildren and eight great-grandchildren. She will enjoy a personal demonstration of owls by a lady who will bring them to Hays to entertain the residents! Old friends are invited.

July 2014

Ray and Patsy Smith – a trip to Brittany

When we bought Wallmead Farm in 1949 only two of the cottages were actually on the farm. Fred Rogers, the dairyman, lived in the Dairy Cottage close to the farm buildings and Bill Cornick, the foreman, lived with his large family in Haygrove on the top of the hill. They had no electricity and no proper road served the cottage. The water supply was shared with the Frys' cows.

We soon built Jobbers Cottage for a succession of farm managers and Haygrove was available to let on the open market. People living there had to be rather adventurous and two of the last tenants were Ray and Patsy Smith. Ray fixed up a little wind generator which stored electricity in a bank of post office accumulators. These could give feeble television reception for a few hours in the evening when Ray returned from his pioneering work with the *Blackmore Vale Magazine*.

Perhaps it was the primitive conditions in Wiltshire, but Ray and Patsy decided to live in France, buying a three-storey period house in Dinan in Brittany. It is in the Rue du Petit Fort, a precipitous cobbled street, like Gold Hill but half a mile long, leading from the centre of the town to its port on the river Rance. This proved for our family to be an excellent holiday venue for several years from 1988 onwards when most of our children were at secondary school.

This year, 25 years after our last stay with Ray and Patsy – Ray having sadly died many years ago – Jenny and I decided to return to the Rue de Petit Fort for a nostalgic visit to all the places that we had known. We found a little gîte a short distance away with a very welcoming landlady from New Zealand, and had a wonderful two weeks. Lots of restaurants and cafes, no Starbucks etc.

Brittany is like a larger version of Cornwall and the farming is similar. As there are no fences or hedges anywhere, including along the TGV railway line to Paris, the farming is all visible from the road. No cow parsley grows on the verges and I only saw one nettle. We saw no outdoor pigs and no sheep. The fields were being cultivated, as ours were when we left, for forage maize, and zero grazing, where the cows never go out to grass, is practised for the many dairy herds which provide milk for the local cooperatives. Brittany is far more forested than our West Country and I did not see that the farmers had left any field margins for wildlife. There were groups of the usual tall wind turbines turning lazily along ridges, but no solar panels on buildings or anywhere else.

We took a short train journey in a solitary diesel carriage which operates a shuttle about five times a day between Dinan and the lines to Paris. It swayed slowly along the single track. Dinan station is a most impressive 1930s building which was a major junction and could still accommodate 12 carriage trains. There are many overgrown sidings and a permanent staff of about four!

The French are very patriotic in their choice of cars, Peugeots and Citroens, and conservative too in their choice of colours: grey. Our exploration of the coast (we were sometimes the only people on the beach) included stumbling across many of the concrete installations of the Atlantic wall built by slave labour between 1940 and 1944. It may have been these years of occupation by the Germans which meant that the products of the Bayerische Motoren Werke have not achieved the same popularity with the French as with the British. In any case, cars in France are more modest with very few SUVs.

For the first time our visit coincided with one of the famous 'pardons' which are held annually in some of the more religious areas of western Brittany. The one we attended was at Treguier, a small city, rather like St Davids in Wales, with a historic cathedral. Nearby is the birthplace of Saint Yves, a 12th-century bishop who loved justice.. The *pardon* is an act of repentance by the local community and in particular the legal profession. The procession from the cathedral included dozens of lawyers in court dresses together with their judges with very decorative hats and gorgeous robes. As the *pardon* is also dedicated to the poor, I hoped that the bishop inside the cathedral had given the lawyers a rousing sermon about the need to keep their fees within reach of ordinary mortals.

As the procession came out of the cathedral to the sound of bagpipes and parading the saints' banners of all the local villages, photographs were taken by all and sundry and it turned into quite a festive occasion. The high point was when the treasured skull of Saint Yves was paraded shoulder-high in a special reliquary by at least three bishops. Saint Ives in Cornwall is not the same man; he was a 5th-century Irishman, Saint Ia.

We had time, as we came back for our ferry at Caen, to visit the Normandy beaches and in particular the Mulberry Harbour exhibition at Arromanches, seventy years on. Thirty thousand British people were engaged in constructing these concrete floating harbours for two years before D-Day.

At the same time, tens of thousands of forced labourers were working in France along the whole coast facing us, constructing the Atlantic Wall in concrete. To some extent it was a battle of technology. In the end of course it was the individual going into action at great personal cost who made the difference.

In gratitude I brought back a Breton pebble to place on the site of Ray Smith's ashes, buried on the farm near Haygrove and overlooking Tisbury.

November 2014

Childhood in Alderbury : the war

I was born in the village of Alderbury, three miles south of Salisbury, on 31 January 1937. The Alderbury historians are now appealing for memories from former times but I thought I would try them out on you first as it may encourage reminiscences from those of you who were children of the same age as me during the war.

My sister Rosalind was born in September 1940 so she was only five when the war finished. Before the war, we lived in some luxury. Hillside in Clarendon Road was a large brick-built house dating from perhaps 1910. Its three floors included staff accommodation with a door covered in green baize on the ground floor between the kitchen and other service quarters and the rest of the house. Our father Jack was a partner with Rawlence and Squarey, estate agents and auctioneers in Salisbury. He employed about five members of staff at Hillside which he had inherited from his mother; she gave him the house on his marriage to Daisy Tylden in 1934.

As well as the house we lived in, my parents owned another house next door occupied by the Bennett family who owned the *Salisbury Journal*. Opposite the drive there was a gardener's cottage and beside the A36 was a pair of cottages occupied by another gardener, Mr Latchem and his family and the local milkman, Mr Taylor. The Alderbury historians have recently printed the Taylors' family history.

Houses were heated by coal and wood in those days as oil-fired central heating had not yet taken on. During the war, coal became unobtainable. We had eight acres of garden and my father set up a wood business employing two or three men who were exempt from war service. They gathered cordwood from local woodland where the timber had been taken out for the war effort. This cordwood was then converted into logs in the woodsheds near the house. The screaming noise of circular saws was often present and I was sometimes allowed to go with the men to throw the logs off the ancient lorry into the drives of the customers in Salisbury.

German bombers could be heard overhead on their way to Bristol and chaff used to float down which presumably was to fool the British radar. This was lovely and shiny and collectable. Invasion was threatened and a deep ditch or tank trap was excavated across the south-west of England; it groaned with frogs in their mating season. Part of it ran at the bottom of Clarendon Road where the A36 Alderbury bypass is now. Some of the defences can still be seen if you use the Laverstock rat-run to Tesco; they are close to the humpback bridge over the River Bourne.

I was sent to a dame school in Fowlers Road, Salisbury run by Miss Falwasser. Who can forget such a name? There was no petrol for private cars, which were all jacked up on bricks for the duration of the war, so I used to take the Wilts and Dorset bus. Due to the shortage of petrol this bus was fuelled by gas generated from a coke fire towed behind it on a little trailer. This often proved inadequate for the needs of the engine going up hills. It often stalled on Alderbury Hill on the way back so we had to walk home. The bus could not possibly tackle Pepperbox Hill so it only went as far as the Three Crowns at Whaddon. Timetables were unreliable so when it was ready to leave the Salisbury bus station, you had to listen for the shout 'ALLDENWADDEN'.

Then as now I was very preoccupied with steam engines. The Salisbury to Southampton railway line also ran along the bottom of Clarendon Road. Occasionally we would put a penny on the track and hope to recover it in a bent condition when the train had passed over. However, much more exciting was to walk down Junction Road to the signal box which controlled the single-track line to Bournemouth via Downton. The signalman had a lonely existence and was quite willing to allow me at the age of 10 to help him with his levers and even give the driver of the Bournemouth train the token which allowed him to go onto the line. I could also receive the token from him when the train returned.

Not content with this, I made friends with one of the shunter drivers at Salisbury Station. The express train to Exeter did not stop at Tisbury or any intermediate stations until it got to Templecombe, then an important junction. There was therefore a need for two or three coaches to be put in the bay platform by a shunting engine. This short train would follow the express, dropping off passengers from London, who had changed at Salisbury, at the intermediate stations. We never ventured out of the confines of Salisbury Station but the driver and his fireman would put up with me for hours, collecting carriages and moving them around the yard. The high point was when the driver fried eggs or cooked Welsh rarebit on his shovel in the firebox. Imagine such adventures being allowed these days.

Occasionally when we were in Salisbury, sirens would sound and then we would have to find a place of safety. Many of the shops and surgeries had Morrison shelters like cages which you could lie under or we could hide under the stairs. Most food was rationed so we often visited the British restaurant in Rollestone Street, which later became the Tisbury Press. It had been a swimming bath and a floor had been put over it. Queues of people could line up for a substantial midday meal which supplemented the meagre ration allowances of meat. You can imagine that wartime queues were quite matey and we used to sing the old Vera Lynn song 'Whale meat again' as we waited for this rather exotic substitute for the protein we were used to. We would also visit the market to buy parts of animals which were not included in the ration, such as pigs' heads from which my mother and Maggie made tasty brawn.

My father had been called up in the Air Ministry and he spent the war in the Windwhistle pub on the A30 near Chard. His job was to requisition land for aerodromes in the south-west of England. He was seldom at home although he managed the wood business all through the war.

The nearest we experienced to actual war was when a German bomb landed randomly in the wood opposite our house and a few clods of earth splattered our roof. We had had our own Anderson bomb shelter built at the end of the garden and this featured in our childish adventures. The Taylor boys, Keith and Terry, became very much part of our activities and we played Swallows and Amazons with them. Keith emigrated to Australia and Terry became a colonel in the British Army with an important role in America. The Latchem family was not so interesting to us. Mr Latchem would chase us out of his kitchen garden with his hoe and his daughter Mavis claimed to have a wonderful singing voice, but you can imagine that this was not quite to the taste of any seven-year-old boy.

Eventually the war was to come to an end following D-Day. The American troops were billeted locally in many woods. In order to embark at

Southampton or Portsmouth they came down the old A36 through the village in lengthy convoys. We sat on the bank at the top of Clarendon Road waving Union Jacks and they threw sweets, biscuits and fruit to us, spoiling us rotten.

After the war my father returned to Alderbury. He had always wanted to farm and in 1948 was successful in buying Wallmead Farm from the Wardour Estate. Hillside was sold and most of the grounds have now been developed with houses but the original house is much as it was. Our son John and his family live in Whaddon, so I keep up to date with the goings-on in the village.

May 2015

Thoughts on milk quotas

L ike any business, farms tend to get submerged in paperwork and our filing cabinet is overflowing. It is therefore with great pleasure that I am preparing to get rid of a file called 'Milk Quota'. Milk quotas started in 1984 and were abolished on 1 April 2015.

You may remember that in the decades after the last war, farming became largely mechanised and there was a surplus in the developed world of many products, particularly wheat, milk and beef. So-called 'mountains' and 'lakes' appeared as the surplus production was bought by governments at low set prices and kept in 'intervention stores'. The wheat was stored in buildings and silos, kept dry and in good condition, the milk was made into butter and milk powder, and the beef was frozen. This kept prices even, as the surplus could be sold from intervention into the market as soon as prices picked up a little and demand increased.

Solutions were sought to prevent the mountains and lakes from growing. In the case of milk it was decided to limit production by establishing ceiling quotas for each country in the EU, at the same time reducing the amount of milk which each country was producing by nine per cent. This was based on milk production for the calendar year 1983 and Wallmead Farm was awarded a quota of 762,371 litres, which was equivalent to the production of just over a hundred cows.

The initial price that we were then being paid for the milk was just under 15p per litre and we were compensated at the rate of 27p per litre total, paid over seven years for the production that we were prevented from continuing. If the whole of England went over the national quota in any year then everyone was penalised by a levy. Monthly figures were produced showing how we were doing, with adjustments for the butterfat element of the milk, which in our case was four per cent.

The result of all this was that smaller producers thought about giving up and found to their pleasant surprise that their milk quotas could be sold and were worth a lot of money. If they were tenants, then the quota had to be apportioned between tenant and landlord. Many producers retired from milking cows and kept beef instead. They shared the quite generous proceeds of the quota with their landlord and sometimes retired completely. This was quite a windfall for farm tenants who in the past, with failing businesses, could well have found themselves out of their holding with not even a roof over their head. Milk quotas therefore had mixed blessings.

In our case we were selling milk to the much-missed Milk Marketing Board which was then broken up in the early 1980s. After that we sold to Milk Marque and later to Milk Link, now Arla. (Please continue to buy Cravendale milk and Anchor and Lurpak butter!) The dairy companies handled the complicated maths of the quota system. At Wallmead, we found ourselves having to buy quota from people going out of dairying in order to increase our cow numbers and remain profitable. Over the years we had to invest £100,000 in buying quota in this way. Some quota cost us as much as 40p a litre and this year we have had nearly two million litres of quota.

By 2015 milk production had decreased in England with the retirement of so many dairy farmers. The country was no longer going over quota or likely to do so. Quota became virtually valueless. We needed to shift the £100,000 from our balance sheet. Various businesses sprang up over the country buying and selling quota for farmers and this usually involved the artificial notion that you had to rent grazing on a farm miles away – that you never visited – in order to substantiate the legal transfer of the quota from one farm to another. Imagine the army of civil servants needed to administrate all this! These businesses now bought all the old quota for almost nothing and resold it for almost nothing, plus a margin for them. This created a large book loss getting rid of the balance sheet figure which could usefully be placed against any capital gains.

You'll understand why it is a relief to get rid of a file which is bulging with all these phoney transactions, now relegated to history. The quota regulations affect all the countries in the EU and as they have now been lifted we may expect that some countries will increase their milk production as a result. However, in the case of England, with the very depressed milk price we have at the moment, I cannot see much change. Any hike in production will depress the price still further. The relentless process of the smaller dairy producers going out of business, with production shifted to much larger units will continue. We have geographical limits as our farm is close to the River Nadder, on a sloping site, so we will continue with our basic dairy unit of 220 cows for the foreseeable future.

October 2015

Roads and mapping

I t is hard to remember these days but our local roads were subject to several small but significant improvements after the war. The A30 was straightened between Fovant and the first turning to Swallowcliffe and visibility splays were cut out of the banks at road junctions around Tisbury. I even persuaded the surveyors at Wilton to carry on this work in the 1980s along the Chicksgrove Lane where visibility was very poor and minor crashes were frequent. This involved the cooperation of local landowners who were only too happy to help.

The road surveyor changed. When I suggested more improvements, in particular to blind spots along the road to Wardour, I was told that they were no longer possible, because any improvements to visibility would make cars drive faster.

One of the first improvements involved improving visibility when turning right from Wardour towards Ansty along Jobbers Lane. The acquisition of part of our land for this purpose took in a triangle of the adjoining Wardour allotments. This particular area happened to be the village horseradish patch and so this strong plant has thrived mightily in the road verge ever since. Normally the road verge is as hard as iron by the time that the plants reach maturity in the early autumn. This year, after six inches of rain in July and August, the road verge was quite soft so I dug masses of ancient and very knobbly horseradish roots and have made some of the strongest horseradish sauce that you will ever find. I may be giving away a few jars and I would assure you that they have been diluted with inoffensive Co-op horseradish.

While I was digging, a car stopped and the driver asked the way to Salisbury. I then realised that one of the many lorry drivers, misled by their sat-navs and ignoring the early warning signs about the low three-arch bridge, had backed into the old wooden signpost and demolished it. The only sign remaining is the English Heritage one saying 'Old Wardour Castle 3 miles' which points at our house. This is quite convenient when telling people how to find us. I assumed that the man in the car who wanted to go to Salisbury had neither a map nor a sat-nav so I realise that there are some people without either.

As a former fellow of the Royal Institution of Chartered Surveyors I have always loved maps and take a copy of the relevant section of my journey with me in the car. I really do not like the display of a sat-nav which seems to emphasise the fact that when you're in a car you are totally divorced from the surrounding countryside and its interesting features.

All our maps derive from the work of the Ordnance Survey. I have a set of reproductions of the old series at one inch to the mile covering south central England. The basic surveying of our country was a military operation under the Royal Engineers, begun in 1792 in response to the threat from Napoleon. The first maps published were therefore coastal, starting in 1809 in south Devon, then taking in the Isle of Wight in 1810 and completing the south coast by 1816 – after Waterloo and the demise of Napoleon. As a matter of interest the survey of England and Wales was completed with the Scottish Borders in 1869.

There was a recent telephone television programme about the original surveying process. One of the problems was identifying the name of any small village or hamlet. The surveyors probably had great difficulty understanding local dialects and so they were told to ask only responsible people like vicars or landowners for help. This still produced several spelling anomalies in our particular area: Haygrove appears as Highgrove and Hazeldon Farm sometimes has an s for the z. Swallowcliffe had its final e omitted and Totterdale was written Totteridge.

This original survey was quite satisfactory for many years but before the last war it was decided that a completely new one was needed. This involved peppering the high spots over the whole country with the familiar concrete cones known as triangulation points. The work was started in the 1930s and could not be completed until after the war, in the 1960s. The concrete had to be taken up to the top of each hill by the Ordnance Survey staff and the metal plate affixed to the top. This is the source of the popular maps that we all have for walking and other purposes. However, nowadays new surveying is all done from the air or ground using satellite identification. This is accurate to within inches as we know from the use we make of this technology on our tractors and combines. The trig points are redundant.

If I go to a second-hand shop I always look at the old maps section. There's not much point buying more and more of them, but I do love handling them and enjoying the quality of the paperwork and draughtsmanship. As far as we farmers are concerned, very sophisticated mapping is now used by DEFRA and they regularly produce new plans for us, field by field. Recently Peter established a dew pond in the corner of one of our fields and I had to survey this to mark it on the current maps so that we could not claim a subsidy for cultivating it. I have yet to hear from DEFRA as to whether my draughtsmanship is up to scratch.

August 2016

Thoughts on Brexit

I was one of the last young men to be caught up for National Service at the age of 18. So I signed on after leaving agricultural college and spent two years as a signalman in the Royal Corps of Signals, 18 months of it in Bavaria. Working shifts over 24 hours listening to the Soviet satellites' radio traffic, we had a lot of spare time and became quite immersed in German life and culture.

The Second World War had been over only ten years and we were all very aware of the legacy of two world wars which to us rather naive young men seemed pointless. In order to take part in local events we all learnt a certain amount of German and this, added to my schoolboy French, and Spanish which I studied later, gave me confidence in moving around western Europe with some ability to converse in the local languages.

Through all this I felt that I was a European, proud to be British. It was therefore with some concern that I became aware that David Cameron was calling a referendum on the future of the UK in Europe. I had already met Nigel Farage on two occasions and was not impressed. Our valued Polish farm worker Pawel seemed to anticipate what was coming and so he and his wife recently acquired British citizenship. When I found to my dismay that our local MP Andrew Murrison was a Brexit supporter, I decided to write to my MP for the first time in my life, pointing out what I thought were the main danger points for our country if we left Europe. My arguments did not impress him in the least!

It has therefore been with some horror that I find a clear majority has voted to leave Europe. In particular I am concerned for my grandchildren who are very keen to stay in. The future of the country is in their hands and not those of over-70s like myself.

Many of my points to Andrew Murrison were to do with the future of agriculture. Farmers in this country have been very well supported by the European Common Agricultural Policy which has been far more understanding and generous to us than the British government ever was in the days before we joined the EU. Of the £3 billion which farmers receive annually from Europe, the £80,000 or so which is paid to Wallmead keeps us in business.

The future of the Arla Cooperative in the UK, which is based in Sweden and sources milk from several European countries as well as Britain, must be in some doubt as it relies on the free movement of milk products from this country to the rest of Europe and back. Tariffs could interrupt this and we might find ourselves on our own again with a limited market. In passing, I dread to think what might also happen to the large foreign car manufacturers who have chosen to make their models in this country.

The coincidence of all this happening at the time of the commemoration of the battle of the Somme is particularly poignant to me because of my recent visit to Picardy. There is always a danger that people forget history and the almost continuous confrontations and wars that used to take place between us and our European neighbours. The European Union has at least promoted peace between its members for the last forty years.

I fear that I will be too old to see the outcome of all this and I can only hope that the younger generation will now successfully take on a new and unnecessary challenge to save our country from economic woes. I apologise for being so pessimistic. In my articles in *Focus* I have avoided politics up to now but I felt that I must, for my fears for the future of agriculture, speak out.

December 2016

Becoming a minister : my faith

Afew years ago I reviewed a wonderful book by Richard Dawkins called *The Ancestor's Tale: A Pilgrimage to the Dawn of Life*. Dawkins is one of the leading biologists of our time and writes non-technically about the evolution of man over millions of years. Like Dawkins I am amazed by the variety and beauty of everything around us and I'm curious as to how it all came about. Dawkins, however, upset some of his listeners by the following paragraph at the very end of his amazing book:

> *I do not wish to reduce or downgrade the true reverence with which we are moved to celebrate the universe once we understand it properly. My objection to supernatural beliefs is precisely that they miserably fail to do justice to the sublime grandeur of the real world. They represent a narrowing-down from reality, an impoverishment of what the real world has to offer.*

Many scientists would agree with him that evolution has no obvious evidence of planning, no room for supernatural beliefs and therefore what might traditionally be called God. However, some, like me, cannot quite give up on religion. I find I want to give worth and reverence to the beauty around us and in particular the life and love which we find in people.

I was brought up in the traditional Church of England way at public school where I was confirmed. For several years, when I was living on the farm at Tisbury, I regularly attended eight o'clock communion at St John's. During my two years' National Service in Catholic Bavaria I lost touch with regular worship. When I returned to work at Southampton I spent many lunch hours with Douglas King, an older deeply thinking man who had been brought up as a Methodist. He found their teaching at the time quite rigid and had gently put it on one side. Both of us knew that all religions are man-made, though rooted from some common sense of awe, even fear, and the need to give life meaning. I therefore decided to explore alternatives to Christianity and for many years practised Buddhism. Buddhism does not overtly talk about God but instead talks about the uncreated and the importance of living one day at a time. This is one way of experiencing oneness with all life in the presence of other like-minded people and I still find it attractive.

However, after a conversion experience, in unity with Jenny and encouraged particularly by our rector at the time, Paul Bunday, I returned to mainstream Christianity and was ordained 35 years ago.

I continually meet people who have rejected all religions on the basis that they historically have, and do, cause division and warfare. The evidence is there in every generation and it is a difficult objection to answer.

Some years ago I felt that I would be happier joining in mainly silent worship with people who believed like me in non-violence. I found a home with the Religious Society of Friends, called the Quakers. With the encouragement of our then Bishop I became a Quaker while remaining an ordained member of the Church of England. To use Terry Waite's word as he followed the same path, I became a 'Quanglican'. Quakers believe that there is that of God, or good if you prefer it, in all people.

In his first Reith Lecture last month on Religious Identity, Kwame Anthony Appiah suggests that three interlinked factors are found in those of us who practise any religion together:

A   We find a place of worship that we like being in, and are happy with what we do there.

B   We enjoy the company of people we meet there and do it with.

C   Less importantly, we share beliefs and doubts.

In other words, religion is primarily a social activity. I like the Hungarian proverb: 'Those who believe are happy, those who doubt are wise.' I hope I am both!

The farming year

2010–2016

April 2010

A few choice remarks about the long section of hedge-laying that I was to tackle on Quarry Farm during the winter brought some willing volunteers who wanted to learn the art. Together we laid about 300 metres of thorn over six weeks, struggling to reach the hedge each day through a muddy field of winter turnips being eaten off by store cattle and then the remainder of last year's lambs.

The lambs got mixed up in the brambles we had cut out of the hedge and went off festooned. The ever-changing view from the top of the hill with aircraft and helicopters flying past, the hourly trains and skylarks ascending, were welcome distractions from the hard work. There will be a great bonfire of the heaps of surplus growth; hedge trimmings are the only materials that we are allowed legally to burn in the open. Those smoking allotment fires are now banned!

The grassland looks brown after weeks of frost and food stocks are running low. Thankfully the trade for cattle and sheep has held up well so we decided to sell the 18-month-old cattle that have not been bred for dairy replacements. The last 42 various Friesian crosses averaged about £550 each with an Aberdeen Angus cross steer fetching £758. Three hundred lambs sold in January averaged £71.40 each.

Our milking cows started going out on the dry frozen fields at the beginning of March but there was no grass yet and they just enjoyed the exercise and fresh air after four months indoors. Sadly the milk price is so low that there is no profit in dairying and little hope of improvement in the foreseeable future. In spite of the planned appointment of an Ombudsman to ensure that the ten supermarket groups play fair with suppliers, some of them are still said to be up to their old tricks of demanding retrospective payments and making sudden changes to trading terms.

Although we gave up outdoor pigs ten years ago we still try to buy British reared pork and bacon. This is out of sympathy for a branch of farming which, like chickens, has never received a subsidy and involves hard, smelly work which, because of the cycles of prices, is never certain to make a profit. The labelling is still misleading. Supermarkets can sell bacon labelled 'Produced in the UK' when the sides have come from Holland or Denmark and are processed here, even claiming to be 'Wiltshire Cured'. There is a voluntary code to stop this and the country of foreign origin should be displayed, although in small letters and sometimes still showing a pretty picture of the British countryside! Loyalty may require spectacles and a thorough examination of the packet.

Our local climate is freezing under a prolonged spell of high pressure so tractors can go out on the land to chain-harrow, apply farmyard manure and spread nitrogen to get the grass growing when the ground warms. Soon, no doubt, the Atlantic lows will come in from the south-west, although last year we had to wait until July for the rain to really come and belatedly give us good growing conditions. As ever we are dependent on the weather.

September 2010

The cereal harvest was going well in mid-August but then the drizzle started. The yields of barley, oilseed rape crops and wheat seem to have been surprisingly good considering the very small amount of rain that has fallen since February. The Frys' latest combine is satellite controlled and the other one has a laser which can see the edge of the standing crop and steers itself to cut exactly along the right line. The operator has to turn at the ends of each pass and is insulated inside the air-conditioned cab listening to music; outside is a cloud of dust with tractors and trailers coming alongside to take the wheat away. The bigger combine has a cutting knife over 30 feet wide and the machine itself is too wide for some gateways. Meeting any combines in the lanes can be quite a scary experience and following them can bring on road rage.

The drought in Russia has been much publicised and exports have been stopped to protect the home market, but the extensive floods in Canada have received less media attention as they have affected vast areas of the prairies rather than people's houses. The result is that the wheat acreage in Canada is down to 7.9 million hectares, still an enormous area but the lowest since 1971. These two global factors, with others, have affected the wheat price and already we have seen the price here during August rise by more than 50 per cent from £100 to £160 per tonne. Canada exports the bulk of its wheat crop and half a million tonnes goes to China each year. Canada has also done a deal with Columbia which has upset the American wheat farmers; politics comes into wheat prices as well as the worldwide weather situation. It is the carry-over of wheat stocks which is critical: stocks of over 200 million tonnes means a low price; below 150 million and the price rises. Playing the market for wheat futures is big business centred on Chicago.

The barns at Totterdale Farm will hopefully soon be full of cereals and Matt Fry will again be doing our marketing for us. It can sometimes be almost a year before everything is sold and the last cheque for 2009 feed barley only arrived this July with a most apologetic note about the amount it realised of £83 per tonne. Barley was not worth growing for feed last year but it is almost impossible to estimate the price and yield a year ahead. Some very large farming companies do not gamble on price but sell a large proportion of their cereals forward – even for the harvest after next. Fertilisers and sprays are also contracted in advance so the shareholders can be given fairly accurate cashflow forecasts for the next season.

Global warming seems to have been out of the headlines recently but methane emissions from the back ends of cattle and sheep amount to a significant proportion of greenhouse gases. Experiments have proved that curry can reduce the sheep's methane emissions. Unfortunately only a small part of the sheep's ration is purchased feeds and it is unlikely that our own 700 ewes are going to get a regular curry takeaway. Experiments are continuing with cattle and this may be a more fruitful line of research. The curry could affect the taste of the milk, lamb and beef, so be prepared one day for new promotions in the Co-op.

The cap on workers from non-EU countries has produced problems for seasonal immigrants like shearers. Five hundred come here from Down

Under each summer to shear 15 million sheep. I understand that they will be allowed in next year as people having 'scarce skills'.

I can end on a brighter note as the amount we are paid for the 1.2 million litres of milk we produce each year has edged up by nearly 2p over the last four months. It is still less than the price 10 years ago. However, the grass stopped growing strongly months ago, so silage and hay are scarce and expensive if any has to be bought in.

February 2011

T he fourth quarter of 2010 was the wettest of the year and made a total of 760mm compared with 1,005mm in 2009. Rainfall has been declining in the Nadder Valley each year for several years but it is the timing of the wet months rather than the annual quantity that matters and this is fairly unpredictable. Last year the four wettest months were February, August, October and November. In 2009 they were January, July, November (twice as much) and December. There is a bit of a pattern here but spotting the wet summer month in advance would be a boon to organisers of weddings, fetes and other outdoor events. It would also help us decide when to risk making hay.

The recent snow was a problem for our hundreds of sheep which could not get at the grass for a few weeks and had to be fed with scarce hay which rocketed in price nationally. When I was at Seale Hayne Agricultural College many years ago, the principal thought he could persuade sheep to eat silage which had been made in small bales with wet Devon grass and clamped. The result was a mass of string in contorted skeins which the sheep soon lost interest in: an experiment that was not repeated.

Sheep rely on grass right through the winter and we have plenty of rough grazing on steep ground nearer Wilton which they are happy to pick through between the emmet butts (ant hills). We sold a batch of 140 May-born lambs in December, averaging over £70 a head. The outlying cattle also compete for grass and expensive concentrates so in January we sold 38 young store cattle of various breeds crossed on the Friesian dairy cows at an average of £360 a head. Many farmers give up milking cows each year and, if they continue as beef farmers, buy store cattle like these during the winter to fatten in the summer.

How long it is possible to milk cows at a loss is a big question for us all. The price we are paid by the Milk Link Cooperative is about to increase to 26p a litre in February, still below most farmers' cost of production. We have invested so much in our 180 cows and, while Peter is prepared to get up at 4.30am to milk them, we will continue. I don't know how he does it and he doesn't know how I could conduct over a hundred funerals last year!

I was pleased to meet Jimmy Leaney and his family from Cornwall who had come up to a family funeral recently. Jimmy had worked at Wallmead for years as a boy and knows quite a few stories about 'the two Teds' – Ted Woods and Ted Rixon, my father's original farm workers. Jimmy told me that at my 21st birthday party in the Victoria Hall my father had approached Ted Rixon with a plate of food and a serviette. Ted had never seen a serviette before. Having looked at it doubtfully, he loyally said, 'Well boss, if you're going to eat one, I suppose I can too.'

September 2011

When we came to Wallmead in 1949 we took over the small Shorthorn dairy herd from the previous tenant farmer, Miss Doggrell. We also inherited her two dairymen, Fred Rogers and Jackie Ingram. Within a year or two, as part of a national scheme, our cattle had to be tested for bovine TB. Every dairy farm had to be isolated from its neighbour by double fencing for several years. Many cattle 'reacted' and had to be slaughtered during those early years but by the end of the 1960s most herds throughout England were getting clear tests and by the mid-1970s the whole country was free of bovine TB. The exceptions were pockets in Cornwall and Gloucestershire where a few reactors were still found. We had no reactors for over 30 years. All milk was proudly advertised as coming from TT (Tuberculin Tested) herds and most of it was pasteurised.

Overcrowding and insanitary conditions in the cities in the 1900s had led to a high incidence of often fatal TB in humans. The rising demand for milk was being met by producing milk from infected cattle and milk was then unpasteurised. As a result of the cattle testing and eradication programme together with improvements in sanitation, TB in humans has become uncommon.

Soon after the virtual eradication of bovine TB and quite independently, the Badger Act in 1973 was brought in to protect badgers from badger baiting. The law was beefed up in 1992 with the Protection of Badgers Act which also made it an offence to disturb a badger sett. Previously badgers had been controlled like deer, rabbits, foxes, pigeons, crows, magpies and other so-called vermin by farmers and gamekeepers, and so there was a small but healthy, well-distributed population of badgers. With the new legal protection badgers had no predators at all apart from the motor car.

I understand that the enormous increase in bovine TB in cattle during the last 20 years has been linked scientifically to the greatly increased badger population. The problem is that badgers, like people living in insanitary overcrowded conditions in cities, are liable to pass on the disease from one to another. When a badger becomes ill with the disease it often leaves its sett and will wander into the vicinity of livestock buildings to try to feed itself until it dies. In 2009, 36,000 cattle reacted to the test and had to be slaughtered at a cost to the taxpayer of over £108 million. This was an increase of 33 per cent on the previous year.

During the last two years, our dairy herd and several of our neighbours have had single mature cows reacting to the bovine TB test. Post-mortems have never shown clinical evidence of TB; the test only shows that the animal has been in contact with the bacillus. Each one has had to be destroyed and the whole farm put under quarantine for 60 days until the next test. Unfortunately our re-test last month identified another reactor, a pregnant cow in her prime. We are now looking into ways of isolating some of our land from the dairy herd at Wallmead so that cattle that we need to sell can be reared in isolation units where they can be tested clear for sale.

We've seen an enormous increase in bovine TB reactors, mainly in the south-west of England and particularly in Gloucester. If any trials are to take place involving the control of badgers it will not be anywhere near south Wiltshire. We are now watching the politics to see whether any steps will be taken by our government. The Republic of Ireland has already started regulating their badger population and the number of reactors there has been reduced by 30 per cent in recent years.

October 2012

We have been amazed by the display of the white and red poppies at Place Farm and adjoining fields on the Fonthill estate to the east of Tisbury. Now that the crop has been harvested, I am able to tell you that the white poppies were grown under licence by Velcourt Farming for morphine production. The morphine is held in the capsule at the neck of the poppyhead. Poppies are a good 'break crop'. Although wheat is usually the most profitable, it cannot be grown repeatedly and a break crop is needed which is often the yellow oilseed rape. In this case Velcourt opted for poppies which are not as profitable. Richard Williamson tells me that the crop was not particularly successful: very heavy rain 'capped' the soil surface so the number of plants that came up was greatly reduced and some fields had to be re-sown.

Red poppies will come up every time that land is cultivated deeply and are intruders. They could not be sprayed because the spray would also kill the white poppies but they produced a beautiful colour. Red poppy seeds appear to remain dormant in the ground for generations.

In order to understand the very difficult growing conditions and tricky harvest, it is worth remembering that the rainfall for the first three months of 2012 only totalled just over 100mm, half of which fell in January. Then came the deluge from April to June when 350mm fell and we've had a further 220mm in July and August. The papers were full of the news that it was the wettest summer on record. Bearing in mind that our total rainfall for the year averages about 750mm, it has nearly all fallen already!

Matt Fry at Totterdale Farm comments that the harvest seems to get more and more difficult to gather each year. The crops this summer refused to ripen due to cold temperatures and moist soils. Yields are well down and on our stony ground we have averaged about two tons of wheat to the acre. A good yield would be double this. The only crop that has done well has been winter barley which has made malting quality; Velcourt at Fonthill also report a very good result for it.

The real story of the year is the quality of the wheat. Part of the measure of quality is the weight of a bushel. I can remember when the farm possessed a galvanised tub which held exactly a bushel of level soil but now the measurements are electronic. A very low bushel weight results from the ears of wheat being extremely small and pinched so the quality is only just suitable for animal feed.

You will have heard of the terrible drought conditions in America, Spain and Eastern Europe. As a result world wheat prices have escalated. We are still not sure what this will mean for our very poor-quality wheat. The straw behind the combine has been so damp that it is questionable whether the large bales of straw will go musty. Matt Fry comments, 'Here's to next year, the sooner this one is over the better.'

The fields are being ploughed again and soon the 2013 crop will be sown. At the same time, on the livestock front, it has been almost impossible to make hay. The maize grown for silage got off to a very bad start and some had to be re-drilled. It is a crop that needs a lot more sun than has been available. We need 1,200 tonnes to go into the silage pit at the beginning of October and it'll be interesting to see if there will be a shortfall. On the other hand the grass has been growing constantly, as anyone mowing a lawn will know, so the cows and sheep have not been short of grass all the summer.

We have only just got rid of all the old season 2011 lambs and now some of this year's May lambs will soon be ready to be sold. Their mothers prepare to receive the attentions of the rams yet again and so the farming cycle continues.

December 2012

From November to March our 200 cows have to be kept indoors as the land would be severely damaged if they were allowed outside to graze the grass. During this long winter period they have to be fed large quantities of bulk material. This is made up of the grass silage which has been made from May onwards, and maize silage which is made all in one cut, normally in the first week of October. This year we grew 85 acres of maize silage but its growth pattern was extremely irregular due to the very dry conditions when it was drilled and then the excess rain and lack of sunshine as it was meant to mature. It was therefore not until about a month after the normal harvesting time that we were able to get to the fields. All around the country there were scenes of desperation as forage harvesters and tractors struggled to cut and macerate the crop and carry it to the clamps in the buildings.

Extra tractors were sometimes needed to pull the tractors and trailers out of the field and sometimes only a half load could be carried. The roads became plastered with mud and in any case the quality of the maize had already suffered. We had the additional problem caused by the closure of the Court Street Bridge so each load from Teffont had a ten-mile diversion. We will now have to see whether what we have harvested will be sufficient for the cows over the winter.

I wrote last month about the extensive steps we have taken to encourage and protect farmland birds, but there is a curious lack of some common birds which cannot be due to any change in farming practice in this area. The ducks in the Nadder next to our house have disappeared; normally there would be about thirty or forty coming hopefully to be fed with peanuts on the drive. On the other hand the large local flock of sparrows is thriving as are the many varieties of tits and especially goldfinches, which seem to be partial to sunflower hearts as well as the tiny niger seeds.

We have been working on the farm budget for next year. The yields of wheat, barley and oats are most difficult to predict due to the swings of climate; the prices we may obtain for them may also vary by about thirty per cent. We may not even be able to sow the wheat seed this winter as the ground is so wet.

Thankfully we have not had a reoccurrence of bovine TB on the farm but the Welsh farmers are getting desperate. Close to 75,000 cattle have been slaughtered in the principality as a result of bovine TB in the last ten years, with 5,000 slaughtered in the first six months of this year. Instead of the temporary eradication which had been proposed by the Welsh Assembly, they are now undergoing a £5 million trial badger vaccination programme in north Pembrokeshire only.

In England the pilot culls in Gloucestershire and Somerset which should have started by now have been postponed until next year. *Countryfile*'s Adam Henson's rare breed cattle have been severely affected by the disease and no doubt he will be anxiously awaiting the result of the pilot next summer.

I appreciate this is a very emotive subject but we dairy farmers feel under considerable threat from bovine TB and we do hope that a solution is found to the problem soon, one way or the other.

June 2013

Farm animals

T he relationship between those who work on the land and animals on a farm is rather different from that between domesticated animals and their owners. We have never kept dogs so I'm not really knowledgeable about the way in which personal relationships build up between dogs and people. I know that these can be very strong and valuable and that each can rely on the other in a very special way.

I have also never kept a horse so I'm not aware of the subtle relationship between horse and rider, and I am always rather surprised that a professional jockey can have an instant rapport with a horse which he (or she) only meets for the first time in the paddock just before a race gets underway.

When we first started farming each of the dairy cows had a name and they were identified purely by their markings. We took over the Shorthorn herd from Miss Doggrell and I still have the book where the names of cows and calves are recorded. There was the usual Daisy, Blossom, Handsome and so on. Then we started crossing the reds and roans with a Dutch Friesian bull and gradually they turned black and white, giving rise to such names as Opal. At the time I was one of the few people who could identify the cows individually. Their names did not matter much to start with but when milk recording came in, the milk recorder had to be told the name of each cow when they came to write down their yield. This could be difficult as we bred from our own cows and kept the mother's name. 'That one's Opal 51 and next to her is Handsome 58.' When we started breeding pedigree British Friesians, each calf had to be sketched on a card which was returned to the breed society. The black-and-white markings were like fingerprints, individual to each animal.

Eventually freeze branding came in. Liquid nitrogen brands painlessly damage the black pigments in each cow's posterior leaving white numbers for the rest of its life. Names then disappeared. More recently, every cow has to have individual yellow plastic recognition numbers in each ear. However, some dairymen have continued to give names to cows that stand out from the others for some reason – especially their favourites.

Interesting situations can occur when young members of the farming family 'adopt' calves and tame them to follow them on a halter. The calf loses all fear of people for life and this can lead to problems as they get older. When the calf becomes a heifer and is out in the field she may exhibit rather too much familiarity with passing walkers. When she gets into the milking herd she resists being driven with the others and will tend to come up to have her back rubbed. It is extremely difficult to move a full-grown, half-ton cow by gentle persuasion.

Recently one such cow, number 65, has been given the name Dolly and comes up to anyone who expresses any interest. Dolly has a particular fetish for the farm dustbins. When the herd goes past them on the way to the field, Dolly will start licking a dustbin in a very determined matter, often turning it over if it is empty, causing all the other nearby cows to jump. Several others seem to have taken on the habit as well. I have no idea why a Wilts Council empty dustbin should excite such interest in a cow. Perhaps someone can tell me why!

Even when cows had names, they never answered to them as far as I could tell. Sheep can be similarly tamed. Nowadays we are quite efficient in persuading a ewe with one lamb to adopt a triplet lamb but a few years ago it was quite common for the triplet lambs to be brought indoors and bottle fed. These became very tame indeed and would follow people round, baaing for their bottle. When I took a family service on the theme of The Good Shepherd, I used to borrow two lambs and bring them into church. One was a tame lamb which came with its human child in tow and a bottle; the other was a normal 'wild' lamb. The two were released in the church simultaneously and the tame lamb naturally sought out its child and had a good suck at the bottle. The other lamb ran wildly round the church, pursued by churchwardens with dustpans and brushes. The theme of the service was of course Jesus' words, 'My own sheep know my voice.' I could only use this trick once in each church but I can remember the procedure taking place at St John's, as well as Hindon, Chilmark and East Knoyle.

September 2013

The barley harvest started about three weeks late and has been going well. Good quantities of valuable barley straw have been baled and stored. Oilseed rape and wheat will follow. The yield in the first big field was about three tonnes per acre. The field at Hazeldon Farm at Wardour has a very difficult soil change at the southern end. It was impossible, due to the wet spring, to drill the barley here at the same time as the rest of the field so the combine will have to come back to harvest it later. This may be a nuisance when the machine has to be brought back from possibly a distant part of the valley through the narrow lanes. The Frys' two vast combines will harvest an area of about 4,000 acres for many local farmers; to do this they will need to cross the railway line several times, often going through Fovant or as far as Barford St Martin to avoid the low or narrow bridges. When the railway line was built in 1850 everything was still being done with horses and most of the bridges only allow for this.

The combines as well as the tractors are regulated by satellite and it's amazing to see the combine driver working for hour after hour without his hands on the steering wheel. This means that he can pay perfect attention to speed and the height of the cutting knife. The result is a much more even cut. It is also interesting that any modern combine can cut and thrash corn when it is going along a slope. Imagine trying to sieve when you're holding your sieve at an angle of, say, 25°. Combines have been designed so that the thrashing mechanism tilts and remains level.

Although the satellites now direct the combine and tractor extremely accurately across the field, attention has to be paid to the presence of poles carrying electricity or telephones, and trees with overhanging branches. A few years ago a tractor drove straight into an electric pole at Berwick St John, putting the whole village out of electricity for 24 hours. This had nothing to do with a satellite – the driver had fallen asleep at the wheel!

Animal health continues to be the big problem with a large dairy herd such as ours and indeed our large sheep flock. In connection with the dairy, there is a prevalent disease called bovine virus diarrhoea (BVD) which can in theory be eradicated if all herd owners take the necessary steps. The disease causes infertility and stunted growth among other problems. If left unchecked, the whole herd will gradually be infected with it. Milk yields will decrease and animals will suffer.

The presence of the disease is sub-clinical and therefore there are no obvious symptoms. It can be present in over 70 per cent of the animals. Vaccination is available but the danger is that a few calves may be born persistently infected (PI) and become a reservoir of the virus. These have to be diagnosed immediately they are born. Virtually the first thing that happens when a calf is born is that a tiny plug of cartilage from both ears has to be removed to enable the yellow identifying plastic tags to be attached. In the case of Friesian heifer calves which are to be replacement cows, the resulting minute piece of ear is then sent to the laboratory for testing; if the calf proves to be PI it must be culled. In this way herds in Scandinavia are now virtually free of the disease but much work needs to be done in this country to eradicate it. I suppose this comes under the old adage: you have to be cruel to be kind.

January 2014

During the autumn I have given two talks on 'Sixty years of farming in the Nadder Valley' to the men's breakfast at Pythouse Walled Garden and to women who lunch at the Wyndham Arms at Dinton. Both were well attended and I fielded questions afterwards:

The EU

I was asked whether in my opinion the European Union was good for farming.

I gave an unqualified yes to the question. Just a few weeks ago we received our cheque for over £80,000 from the Rural Payments Agency which is our share of the annual subsidy paid to all farmers in Europe by the EU. It is based on the acreage farmed and modified by the amount of work we do to preserve the ecological value of our land.

Without the subsidy, mixed farmers like us would be out of business. The last time that our government ceased supporting farmers was in the 1930s when many were bankrupted. Land could not be let and the term 'dog and stick farming' was coined to describe the sort of prairie management that became common.

GM crops

I was asked whether I was in favour of the genetic modification of crops.

Again my answer was yes. We are told, although it is challenged, that we must double world food production by 2050 both to feed the expanding world population and also to meet the increased demand for meat and other luxury foods expected by rising middle classes in places like China.

I believe that there is no health risk to either animals or humans from eating GM food. The history of these modifications goes back to 1875 when wheat was crossed with rye. In 1994, tobacco was approved in Europe which had been modified to resist herbicide and in 2000 a variety of rice was modified called 'golden rice' which has a very high nutrient value. The main benefit from genetic modification is to make a crop resistant to a cheap, harmless weedkiller called Roundup so that it does not have to compete with weeds.

There seems to be anger against firms such as Bayer, Syngenta and Monsanto which have led the development of these techniques. Would we be angry in a similar way with these companies or others that develop new pharmaceutical products to the benefit of us all?

Fifteen million farmers in 29 countries are now using GM seed. The question was asked as to whether this was making the big chemical companies rich at the expense of small farmers. The fact is that small farmers can continue to use their own seed – there is nothing to stop them – but already on a farm like ours we are faced each year with two realities:

- Firstly if we grow forage maize, which is a hybrid, we have to buy new seed each year as the maize seed is non-viable.

- Secondly if we re-use wheat seed we have to pay the original plant breeder a royalty fee for using the variety which that firm has developed at enormous cost. It is a little like buying our replacement sheep from Yorkshire: you cannot go on breeding from the same stock year after year.

In passing I noted in a book I was reading about early railway lines, that the connecting of the populations of villages to their neighbours in Devon in the 1850s had done much to reduce human inbreeding, which used to produce so-called 'village idiots'.

Plant breeders are at the leading edge of technology and I can see no reason to blunt their research into genetically modified food which can only be to the benefit of everyone.

June 2014

Several pairs of lapwings on the farm have hatched their eggs and are being followed around by their grey-and-white fluffy chicks. They make very tasty snacks for predators so we surround their nesting site with an electric fence powered by solar panels. This keeps foxes and badgers away but threats from overhead are more difficult to counter. Crows and magpies are probably the worst but are well known to be clever. Shooting is an option but it is very time-consuming and doesn't seem to reduce numbers sufficiently to make a difference. If you're good at spotting crows and magpies you will see the extent of their numbers the next time you're out in the countryside.

A more effective method of dealing with them is the Larsen trap which we have rather reluctantly started to use to control them. These are wire cages baited with enticing cat food. They work best when a live crow, which becomes very well fed, is placed in the inner cage. This bird will attract others whose natural curiosity will bring them close and possibly entice them into the cage, after which they can be humanely despatched. This is done under a general licence approved by the RSPB. The traps are inspected every day but unfortunately we have found on two occasions recently that some well-meaning person has opened the trap and let the captive crow escape. Indeed this took place away from footpaths, so the person taking this action was trespassing.

I thought it was worth explaining why we use these traps as people may feel the method is inhumane. However, in my mind it is better than shooting. They will only be in use for a short period during the nesting season. We are hoping that, if we can achieve some meaningful reduction in the crow population, we will also see a better success rate from the lapwing project. I'm sure that the crow population will bounce back as soon as we and others stop controlling them.

The wet weather continued until the end of April and we had a dry window in the first week of May which enabled us to make a good start planting the forage maize. The grass has been growing apace and the cows have been out eating it, although the wet conditions mean that the gateways have become a quagmire.

By the time you read this, we shall have been away in Brittany for two weeks and as always I will be interested to see how the local farmers there are coping. The climate is of course very similar to the south-west of England, so we are taking our brollies.

October 2014

Farming is like snakes and ladders. The world population increases and we find ourselves exporting large quantities of milk products, lamb, beef and cereals. The prices go up, production increases; there is then an equilibrium as stocks build up and prices come down again. We are used to this and recently the price for our two million litres a year of Wallmead milk has increased to 35p a litre. Then the snake arrived in the form of Mr Putin's alleged involvement in Ukraine. His reaction to the resultant sanctions by the EU and other countries mean that our precious milk products can no longer be sent eastwards. The EU are making provisions for cheese and skimmed milk powder to be stored pending easier times, but meanwhile our milk prices have suddenly declined by about twelve per cent and are likely to go lower; below the cost of production.

Efficiency becomes more and more important and this means continuing to improve the health of our dairy cows. There are various diseases they are prone to which I have reported on over the years but the two main threats to their health are mastitis (a disease of the udder) and problems with their feet.

We have an excellent chiropodist who comes with his specialist equipment every few weeks. The cows' legs have meanwhile been colour marked to show where any lameness has been noted and he sets to work holding each cow securely while he sorts out their problems. In July he treated 42 hind feet. This lameness is largely due to cows having to walk on hard surfaces such as concrete; even worse is a loose stone surface where they can pick up sharp stones.

Our dairy buildings are built on a slope and it has always been a problem to move cows safely on the sloping concrete without them slipping. This summer we have covered much of the collecting yard with very expensive rubber matting. These, like the mats which we put on top of the silage, are made from recycled tyres. We will see how long they will last. They have to be strong enough to take the tractor and scraper which cleans the yard surfaces twice a day.

During September I was able to visit a dairy farm near Lulworth in south Dorset. J.S. Cobb and Sons have been farming in the area for nearly ninety years and from traditional mixed livestock and arable enterprises they have evolved into specialist dairy farming, taking the care of cows to a very high level. They milk four thousand cows in total which are kept across a number of dairy units. I was interested to see that the milking on a 500-cow unit we visited is carried out three times a day. The milkers work in teams of three doing eight-hour shifts. Out of a total of 19 people engaged in the milking only one is British, the rest coming from Eastern Europe. This is not surprising as we have found ourselves that there are very few local people prepared to undertake such a demanding, dirty and socially awkward job in spite of the financial rewards being substantial.

The dairy unit in question was on a level site and there was a lot of rubber matting. The cows are milked in a thirty-point rotary parlour with 30 milking points rotating. We all stood on the parlour and when it rotated it felt as though the building was going round and the machine we were standing on was stationary. A strange sensation. These particular cows were pedigree Holstein and very carefully bred. They average 12,000 litres of milk a year compared with our 8,000.

By comparison, you may have seen on *Countryfile* that a few miles away the Foot family in Dorset, who started farming with little capital, have built milking parlours on trailers which they move every day – a healthy, outdoor job in all weathers. They only milk their cows once a day so the average milk yield is about 4,500 litres but they keep costs to an absolute minimum. Their milk contract is with a local cheese factory where a steady price is guaranteed. This may be a model for the future but only on well-drained land.

The same day we visited a new anaerobic digester situated close to the Prince of Wales's development at Poundbury, just west of Dorchester. This digester takes in forage maize, hybrid rye and waste from a cereal factory and a chocolate factory. It was the first unit in the world to turn these materials into gas to be fed straight into the main rather than being made into electricity. I believe the capacity of the unit is equivalent to 2MW, sufficient to heat all of Poundbury during the winter and provide excess gas for the main for the rest of the year. However, in order to grow enough forage maize the operators have to rent a large area of land within a 20-mile radius of Dorchester. They pay about £200 an acre rent for the land and this is distorting farm rental values throughout that area. We would not wish to pay more than about £90 an acre rent to take on additional land and therefore could not hope to compete with a business like that if one was to be set up in our area.

When we bought Wallmead Farm, we acquired with it 1.4 acres of allotments at the road junction of Jobbers Lane and the Wardour road. These allotments had been allocated by the Arundell estate to people who lived in Wardour. One can imagine that over the decades beforehand they would have been very busy as farm labourers and other people on very low wages struggled to support their families by producing their own food. The numbers of people interested in continuing dropped off in the 1950s and 1960s. Eventually just one of our farm workers, Wilf Rasen, was left working the remaining quarter of an acre; when he gave up, most of the allotments fell into weedy disuse.

However, during the last 15 years they have been enthusiastically worked by about ten different gardeners and during the summer the area is a hive of activity. At the moment, autumn raspberries of several different varieties are producing heavy crops and there is still masses of food being produced prior to the winter. We have a vacancy at the moment so if anyone is interested in taking on one of these allotments, please phone me on 870 208.

September 2015

The milk price is still very much in the news and Morrisons in particular have found themselves under scrutiny with some blockading by tractors. When I went into the Co-op the other day the staff were worried that I was going to buy their milk and tip it down the drain, but I was only going to buy some of our own milk under the Arla label of Cravendale. I paid £1.19 for a litre of blue top; Arla paid us an average of 24p a litre for our June milk. Some of it was in excess of the standard quantity that they have agreed to buy from us and for this they paid us only 16p, which is about half of the cost of production. Our contract with Arla is a comparatively good one but other farmers are not so lucky and the pressure to go out of business is extremely high.

A recent article in *The Times* suggested that traditional British dairy farmers are very uncompetitive; their problem is that they are producing milk at much too high a cost. The writer recommended mega dairy farms milking presumably about five thousand cows in order to bring the cost down to world levels. I think the public have already shown that they are not keen on this.

Peter and I recently visited another farm with robot milking machines. This was on the very heavy clay land in the Blackmore Vale between Shaftesbury and Sherborne where in any case the cows can normally only graze outside for four months a year. Keeping robots means that the milking cows stay in all the time although they are allowed out for their two-month dry period if it is in the summer and the land is dry. Each robot can milk up to sixty cows. Any more and there are problems.

Cows, like us, cannot stand queuing. Faced with a queue to be milked by the robot, they will lie down as they prefer not to be milked rather to wait any longer. This means that the number of cows on each farm is limited by the number of robots and avoids the temptation, which we have all succumbed to, of gradually increasing cow numbers to try to make a profit. These cows were each given a neck collar which recorded much useful information, relayed to the farm office computer. A microphone in the collar recorded the amount of time each cow spent chewing the cud. Too little can mean a health problem needing attention.

In our case we only pay rent for about half of the thousand acres which we farm and at the moment we have virtually no borrowing. We therefore compare in cost favourably with those farms where rent is paid for all the land and there is substantial borrowing on top of it. If and when interest rates go back to their usual rate of about 8%, those who have borrowed money for recent improvements will begin to suffer even more.

In addition we are a family farm where Peter still does the bulk of the milking himself. If you can find a full-time dairyman you have to pay a lot of money, provide a free house and pay many of his expenses. Getting up at 4.30am every morning and milking until seven in the evening is a lifestyle that does not suit many people.

Harvest is progressing between rainy spells and the yields are looking good. Jasper, our son-in-law, has grown 12 acres of Maris Widgeon wheat at Teffont in order to provide a local thatcher with straw. This variety was especially developed in 1964 for the quality of its straw for thatching. The sight of the sheaves in the field excited local photographers. The 'hiles', as they are called locally, recalled loved and now virtually vanished sights and are emblematic of harvest time in the old days.

July 2016

S hepherding sheep can be a lonely experience. However, the National Sheep Association runs regional shows which bring together everyone in the sheep industry. There are demonstrations of shearing, sheepdog trials, trade stands and competitions. Many of the varied sheep breeds in the country are represented.

To our astonishment, the NSA South Sheep Show took place on 7 June this year at Pouldens Farm at West Hatch. It was hosted by Sir Henry Rumbold and much work was put in by Paul Aldridge and his staff. I only knew about it when the signs went up at the corner of Jobbers Lane the week before. People came from all over England. Important technical seminars took place in a marquee. There were prominent speakers from the Brexit and Stay-in campaigns. Trailer rides enabled visitors to enjoy our beautiful valley.

On entering the showground we came face-to-face with a long open-sided trailer on which stood nine breeds of sheep arranged rather like an Olympic awards ceremony. You can see them online. Look for 'The Sheep Show'. A very lively New Zealand shepherd gave a fast running commentary about all nine breeds on show. His audience included Semley school children sitting right in front. Although his chat was educational, he was brilliant at involving the children, particularly when a ewe shot out of a concealed doorway straight at them. She was expertly rugby tackled by the shepherd before he sheared her. He had a mock auction of the fleece and took the bidding up to £25. He then pointed out that it was probably worth about £1.50, which would be the cost of shearing it. The show ended with a sheep dancing display!

Two of the breeds represented on the trailer were the Blackface from Scotland and the Bluefaced Leicester. These are crossed together to provide the 'mule' and there was an example of this as well.

Fifteen years ago we were able to take a tenancy of Manor Farm at Lower Chicksgrove from Granville Davies who had always kept sheep on his farm and expected us to do so. We took over 370 of his ewes and then built them up to a steady 600. They are all mules. Cross-breeding sheep means that you cannot use your own replacements if you want to maintain the same cross breeds. You continually have to buy in new stock from the north and cross them with perhaps a Texel ram, a Dutch breed also represented at the recent Sheep Show.

Some rather special sheep from the Lleyn peninsular in Wales have been making inroads into the English scene during the last thirty years and we are seriously considering going over to them. This breed originated in quite a small area so the pedigree sheep have known families. It follows that, to avoid inbreeding, the individual sheep have to be recorded in their families. I can see that this is going to involve a lot of record-keeping but should not be too much of a problem, as all sheep now have computerised records.

Every aspect of agriculture is involved with change and the breeding of sheep is a prime example. The majority of sheep in this country are crossbred. This means that the original breeds have to be kept separate so that they are available for the commercial flocks.

Everything at the end depends on price and this comes back to the return that we get for our fat lambs when they go to market. Along with practically all agricultural produce, prices have suffered during the last year or two and are probably down 15 per cent on last year. However, the atmosphere at the South Sheep Show at Hatch was optimistic. It was a great meeting of similar people. Sadly, I doubt if it will ever return to a local venue again as we are in fact on the extreme western extremity of the NSA South East region.

November 2016

T he 2008 financial crisis still has a ripple effect and has put many businesses under stress. After the recent Brexit vote the pound has fallen sharply. This is now beginning to push up the price of many imported goods. Agriculture has not been immune from these factors; much of what we buy is imported. We have had to rethink our enterprises in order to survive.

We are livestock-based as nearly half of our thousand acres are in grass, permanent or temporary. Our herd of 220 milking cows and flock of 600 breeding ewes are very much at the centre of our enterprise.

The cows have taken a very bad knock as the milk price went down very fast over a year from about 32p a litre to 18p: well below the cost of production. As a result many dairy farmers here and across Europe have gone out of business. The result has been a considerable reduction in the quantity of milk produced. Accordingly the price has now started to increase but its revival is always very slow and it will take at least six months to get anywhere near covering the cost of production. This means that the performance of the arable acres has come under scrutiny.

As mentioned earlier, many of our rented fields at Teffont and Chicksgrove have very thin soils over stone and the yields of cereals on a number of fields hardly justify the cost of planting the crop. We are therefore having to look very carefully at each field. The poorest will have to be sown into grass and fenced for sheep for the first time. The ewe flock will be increased.

It will not then be economical to carry a full range of machinery to cultivate the remaining arable fields. We are intending that neighbouring farmers will take some of these over and we will then dispense with our biggest tractor with the specialist drills and other implements that go with it. Sadly, after forty years, we will have to say goodbye to our top tractor driver Alan Porter.

These decisions have been difficult and have involved very hard decisions following a lot of budgeting. The future after Brexit is uncertain, although the government has promised that the present level of essential subsidies will continue until 2020. After that, the future is unknown. If support from our government is less than we have received from Europe, we will have to do some more soul-searching if we are to continue farming.

For the time being, business is as normal. The harvest is finished and we have sown all the winter crops. There is sufficient preserved food for the cattle to keep them through the winter and many of the May-born lambs are ready to sell. Recent rainfall has been slight so the cattle are still out grazing the fields but very soon the leaves will be down, the rains will fall and all the cattle will come in to be housed for the winter.

Postscript

In writing these notes for *Focus*, month after month, season after season, I feel a great and enduring bond with this place in Wiltshire where I have spent almost all my life. Through living, working and farming here I have absorbed its history, its people, its traditions, its ways... and above all the landscape itself.

I seem where I was before my birth, and after death may be.

from *Wessex Heights* by Thomas Hardy

Eventually this place will, as the poet's words imply, re-absorb me, and I will become part of it as it has become part of me. Although not for some years yet, I hope!

This little book is my own personal tribute to Tisbury and to this beautiful corner of Wiltshire. I hope it will evoke, for those who read it, the changing times through which I have lived and the still unchanging rhythms of a farmer's life in 21st-century England.

The compilers of this book have selected those articles which belong to life here. Lest you think I am too parochial, I have written many others based on our travels and my wider interests. My *Farming Notes* continue to appear every month in the parish magazine. There is still so much to write about.

Martin Shallcross, 2017